PERSONAL FINANCE FOR TEENS

A SIMPLE GUIDE TO MONEY BASICS: 7 PROVEN
STRATEGIES TO MAKE, KEEP AND MULTIPLY MONEY

ACHIEVE FINANCIAL INDEPENDENCE AND AVOID
BEING DEAD BROKE

G.G. CUNNINGHAM

CONTENTS

INTRODUCTION

 The more you learn, the more you earn.

— FRANK CLARK

In 2022 Americans reported losing an average of $1,819 just because of a lack of personal finance knowledge. The total cost for adult Americans that year was more than $436 billion because they did not understand or practice many of the basic money strategies outlined in this book.

That same year, 19% of adults aged 25 - 40 reported they certainly could not come up with $2,000 if an emergency arose in the next month.

A recent survey showed that 86% of teens were interested in investing, but 45% said they didn't invest because they didn't feel confident.

The truth is, as a teenager, there is a lot of uncertainty. There is a lot of uncertainty about current situations like school and friendships. But there is also uncertainty about the future—where to go, what to do, and the right decisions.

Being a teenager is difficult, and there is a lot to constantly think about, consider, compare, analyze, and plan. I know the struggle; I've been there myself. And I hope what I have learned can make your journey easier.

Because as a teenager, you're taught a lot of things. You're taught about Pythagoras and what the square root pi is. You know the difference between an adjective and an adverb, and you're taught a lot about history. But how many of those things are you actively using in your daily life? And how much of it will be relevant in the future?

While you're flooded with all this information, nobody in school teaches you about finance and how simple it can be to plan for a good future. And in many cases, like mine and maybe yours, our parents aren't comfortable enough to talk to us about it. So we're left to try and navigate through the world without really knowing what to do to achieve financial success.

We might know that budgets are important and wealthy people invest money. But what does that all mean, and how do you even get started?

Starting with the basics is the first step, which is exactly what this book is about. Helping you understand the fundamentals of finance in a way that's easy to understand and easy to implement immediately. Not only will you be able to start saving money for things like college and your future home, but you will also learn how to run your finances, so it's a smooth process for decades to come.

In this book, you will learn:

➤ The seven most important financial strategies and how to start using them today! These basics include goal setting, earning your own money, budgeting, savings, investing, taxes, and credit.

➤ The most common money mistakes people make and how you can avoid making them. Basically, what not to do.

➤ Additional important opportunities and strategies including cryptocurrency, passive income, how to stay motivated, living within your means, investing for retirement, saving money in a way that can truly elevate the rest of your life, and lots of other tips and tricks to help you develop your money muscle.

➤ How you can plan your path to becoming a millionaire with a normal job!

How to read this book:

- I suggest you read this book a chapter at a time, do the activity at the end of each chapter, and then take a small break.
- Next, go back and reread that chapter before moving on to the next.
- Taking notes along the way is also recommended.

- Be inspired to do additional research if you have more questions.

Why I wrote this book:

I have dedicated my time to creating this book because I want to help teens start their future with financial stability and a solid knowledge base of how money works.

So why the heck is helping you so important to me? Because I know what it feels like to live paycheck to paycheck, to constantly worry about the future, and to never really have enough or be able to plan for the future.

At one point in my life, when I was younger, I was on the brink of bankruptcy, and my debt was enormous. It was an incredibly stressful time filled with anxiety. I don't wish that for anyone else—which is why I wrote this book. I want to help you avoid the common pitfalls and instead start your future with a strong foundation. It's taken me years to gather the knowledge and experience to write this book, and I'm so excited to share it with you. Starting today is going to give you such a tremendous advantage.

These strategies are proven to work. The basic principles that I will teach you in this book are the same ones I used to pick myself up from the brink of bankruptcy, clear my debt, and then build myself a powerful passive income stream that has set me on an unshakable financial path.

You don't have to waste your time learning the hard way with trial and error. You don't have to lose money by making common mistakes. Instead, learn from others like me and set yourself up for dependable success. Starting today when you are young will help you have a better life.

WHAT THE FUTURE COULD LOOK LIKE

Have you ever pictured what your future life would look like? Do you know what things you'll own, where you'll live, who you'll be with, and what job you'll have? I bet it doesn't look like mountains of debt and daily stress over whether you'll get through the month or not. But that is the reality that millions of people face.

You can have that perfect dream life you imagine. You can have certainty and control over your finances. You can be confident about your money and where you put it. You can thrive financially. You can have investments that make you money while you sleep. You can have enough to pay all your bills, take vacations, and still have enough each month to put away in your savings. You can even become a millionaire with a normal job, especially if you start as a teenager. The fact that you're taking the time to read this book already puts you so far ahead of many of your friends and many adults too.

So, avoid being dead broke and create a plan to become a millionaire with a normal job. It is possible, and it isn't that complicated. I'm going to show you all of the tools you need to get there in this book. All it takes is commitment and starting with small, simple steps that I have outlined for you at the end of each chapter.

Remember, starting today is your biggest advantage. The younger you start, the greater your ability to multiply your money—so keep reading! Don't wait until the end of the book, the start of the New Year, or when you're done with school to start taking some action. Start today with small steps and action items at the end of each chapter so you can make your financial success a reality and have the amazing life you're dreaming of!

WHAT THIS BOOK ISN'T

There are so many books that teach you about ways to get rich quickly or teach you about the types of investments that will make you money in an instant. The truth of the matter is that there is no quick fix. There are ways to make quick money, sure. This is not a dependable strategy, though. Instead, take action to build a strong, long-lasting foundation which is truly what you need to be successful. You can't build a house on a shaky foundation. Similarly, you can't build a life on a shaky financial foundation. And so, this book is not about teaching you how to get rich quickly.

Instead, this book is about guiding you through all the basic financial strategies and tools to build that foundation and make the walls of your life unshakable.

1

EYES ON THE PRIZE: SETTING GOALS!

Set a goal and get excited about the possibilities!

Setting financial goals is the first and possibly the most important step to achieving anything with your money. Have you ever heard the saying, "By failing to plan, you are preparing to fail?" When it comes to your money, this is so true.

Setting a goal is about having a vision. It is the first step in making a plan so you can see where you want to go and then figure out what steps you must take to get there. It's so easy to spend money unnecessarily, forget, save, or lose track of where your money is going. Believe me, I've been there! But goals help you see, monitor, and reach your target. And more than that, having a goal will help keep your motivation high, preventing you from spending money on things you don't need and encouraging you to put money aside instead.

But what does that mean? Let's break it down.

1. Financial Goals Help with Planning

As I said, if you're not planning, you're getting ready to fail. It's really that simple. By having an end goal you want to reach, you'll be able to create the necessary steps to get there. For instance, let's say your goal is to buy yourself a new laptop. You know that, realistically, you have to save up money to buy a new laptop. So, by setting a goal of saving up $600 for the computer, you can start planning how to get that money.

These plans can include how you'll make money, where you'll save the money when you buy it, and so on. You can't start planning if you don't know what it's for! So make sure that when setting a goal, you have an exact number you want to save or the exact target you want to reach so that your planning becomes clearer and doable.

2. You Can Start Prioritizing Your Money

Now that you have a goal in mind, you know what amount you're working toward and can create a plan for how to get there. This makes it so much easier to prioritize your money and monitor how you spend it. It's so easy for us to buy Starbucks every weekend or splurge on takeout with our friends without giving it much thought. But the moment there's a goal you know you're working toward, you'll be more aware of where your money is going. So if you know you have to reach $600 in the next few months, you'll be able to prioritize your savings and say no to the small things that will keep you from reaching that goal.

3. You Can See If You've Made Progress

Without a precise goal to work toward, it's tough to know whether you're making progress. Being able to see progress will make you feel more motivated to continue. Think about a project or hobby you've worked on. It's challenging to start and get yourself to work on it regularly. However, when you start seeing the progress, you'll feel more motivated to continue, and the same goes for finances.

If you have a goal, and you see your savings increase and how you're edging closer to that end goal, you'll find it easier to say no to things that will prevent you from saving up that money. Monitoring progress is a huge motivator, and goal setting is the foundation for monitoring progress.

4. You Start Holding Yourself Accountable

One of the greatest lessons to learn as a teen and as an adult is accountability. Simply put, it means taking responsibility for something. In this case, it's about holding yourself responsible for saving money for your goal instead of buying something else. But on the flip side, the remarkable thing about accountability is that you're also responsible for your success. When you finally reach that goal and can buy what you've been saving for, you can pat yourself on the back and know you were responsible for making that happen. It is an incredibly powerful feeling knowing that your actions, goal setting, and commitment allowed for that success.

5. You're Preparing for Adulthood

One of the biggest learning curves that comes with growing up is how to work well with money. It's not something that is taught in school, and most adults aren't doing it well enough to be able to give teenagers advice. So, here you are, heading into adulthood with little preparation for how it all works financially as an adult. You have to instantly learn about income, expenses, taxes, pensions, mortgages, investments, savings, budgeting, planning, and all the rest.

It's a lot to consider at once, but by starting with goal setting and saving, budgeting, and prioritizing, you're already setting yourself up for future success. You will already be a step ahead of so many other teenagers (and, let's be honest, a lot of adults). So, use your budgeting and goal setting as a huge step forward in preparing for the expectations of adulthood.

WHAT SUCCESSFUL GOAL SETTING LOOKS LIKE

Now that you know why goal setting is important and the different areas it will help in, let us look at what an ideal situation for setting goals will look like. Just having a goal of $600 isn't clear enough for you to start planning how to reach that goal, right? So what does a successful goal setting look like to ensure you reach it?

Deciding on a Realistic Goal

Of course, to set a successful goal, you have to decide on the goal. The goal is the end game, the reason *why* you are doing all of this strategizing. So think about what you want to achieve financially. Do you want to save up for something specific? Are you looking to buy something new? If there isn't something specific you want to buy, think about any types of investments you want to try out in your teens. Or if you want a certain amount of money saved for your college fund. Perhaps there's a place you've always wanted to travel to or a car you'd like to buy.

Whatever it is, find that specific thing you want to buy, do, see, or experience and put a number on it. Decide how much you want and when you want it. But most importantly, make it realistic. Are you looking to save up $600 in two months, but you only get a $100 allowance monthly? That doesn't really make sense, so make sure you set realistic goals.

Based on your budget, you will see what is realistic and what is unachievable. If it isn't realistic or achievable, you're bound to lose motivation and give up. So don't aim for something too big right away. This is about getting started so you can learn and see how it works and get excited about the reality of your bigger goals.

Setting a Budget

Based on what you've decided you want to set as a goal, start setting up a budget for yourself. It's about tracking your expenses and money earned—comparing what's coming in versus what's going out. The budget also shows you *where* your money is and how much is in each place. The strategy of tracking your money is key to maximizing its potential.

In Chapter 3, I will break down exactly how to create an effective budget so that you know exactly what to track and how to decide what amount to set aside to reach your goal. Getting started with a budget is easy, but staying motivated to stick to it is the trickier part. However, this is a powerful skill to have and a habit that will greatly benefit you throughout your life. Learning and using budgets is a powerful tool when it comes to money.

Again, a budget is made using your income (what comes in) and tracking your expenses (what goes out). Based on how you've spent money in the past, you will see how much money goes into each category of your life. Within that budget, you will also decide how much money you can afford to put aside for your specific goal. Sometimes it means spending less on other things, but at least there is a clear, realistic plan in mind. The key is to see what you're earning, what you're spending, and what you have left over each month to see what you can realistically set aside for savings.

Creating a Plan of Action

When you have your first goal set and your budget outlined, you should create a specific action plan. The action plan is *what* you are going to do to achieve the goal, which includes your budget, finding income, and other action steps. It's not always enough just to have a goal. You have to have a plan for how to achieve that goal. If you don't have a plan, then you only have a dream with no steps to reach it.

Your action plan will be a lot easier to figure out based on what you have noted in your budget. Your plan can include more ways you're planning on making money or ways you're planning on cutting certain expenses. It will help drive you forward toward your goal and make it clear what steps you have to take to reach that goal.

Some things to add to your action plan may include:

- How much money do I want to set aside each month to reach this goal?
- How much money am I currently getting each month?
- What jobs can I apply for to bring in more money?
- Do I have any items I can sell that I don't need to reach my goal?
- What expenses am I going to reduce, and how will I do that?
- How am I going to create a savings plan so that I can't withdraw for anything except my goal?

Some of these steps include getting a job or selling some of your possessions to earn money, but there are other ways you can make money and increase your income. Don't worry—I will discuss a whole list of diverse ideas for making money in the next chapter, giving you different ideas and options that are doable and realistic for you.

Automate Your Savings

I highly recommend creating an automated savings plan to help you stay on track with your savings. You might need your parents' help at first, so don't be afraid to ask. Technology can work in your favor sometimes, so make use of automated plans to ensure you set aside that money every month. If you never see it, you won't miss it.

This can be done relatively easily on a banking website or app, where you can arrange for a certain amount of money to automatically go into a savings plan without you having to remember to do it every month. This will prevent you from accidentally spending it and ensure the exact amount you budgeted for goes into a separate account. We will look at different savings options in detail in Chapter 4.

Creating a Timeline

When setting a goal, it is really important to decide on a specific date when you want to reach it so that you can better manage your planning strategy. This will also help you monitor your progress and see whether you're on track or not. First, decide when you want to reach the goal. Then create milestone dates that help you check in on your progress along the way and create mini goals within your overall goal. For instance, make a goal to have $300 by October and $400 by November, if your end goal is to have $600 by December.

Your timeline can also include the actions you plan on taking to reach the goal. For instance, in January, you'll find a part-time job; in May, you'll help out at an event for extra money; and in December, you'll wrap Christmas gifts for additional income. Planning what you'll do each month to reach your goal and what amount you want by the end of each month will help you tremendously to reach the end amount.

Reviewing Your Progress Regularly

Create a habit of checking in regularly. Review your goal, plan, and timeline to help you see your progress and whether you are staying on track to meet your final target. Checking in on your progress will not only allow you to adjust your plan, budget, and timeline, but it will also help you stay motivated. When you review your progress and see how much money you're able to set aside, you'll feel more excited and fired up to continue.

There is a lot of power in seeing progress. Be sure to consistently review your plan to keep yourself motivated, psyched, and on track. You should try to look at your progress at least once a month, but the more often you do it, the easier it will be to make adjustments to your plan if necessary. Checking in can become addictive as you continue to see your plan produce results.

Staying Motivated

Staying motivated to continue saving each month is often the most challenging part of saving money. Motivation isn't something that comes automatically, and there will be days when you would rather reward yourself immediately by spending your money rather than keeping it or putting it into savings. This is completely normal, so don't beat yourself up for not always wanting to stick to your plan. Fortunately, there are several ways to stay motivated and on track, even when things get tough. As I just mentioned, reviewing your progress helps boost motivation. Here are some other great tricks to keep yourself motivated:

Use mini milestones.

One of the best tricks to staying motivated is to set up a few "mini milestones" in your plan's timeline and reward yourself for reaching those points along the way to your big goal. The strategy is to build periodic rewards into your plan to boost your motivation and keep you on track. For example, you might plan to buy yourself a pair of shoes when you've reached the $300 mark in your savings. Or, budget to spend a certain amount to go out with friends if you reach the $400 mark.

This way, it won't feel like you're just saving and saving without getting the opportunity to have fun with your money. Remember to keep the amount you spend on these rewards in check with your overall goal. A good rule of thumb is to stay within a 10% range of your overall savings goal for the amount you allocate to these mini milestones. If your end goal is $600, your mini milestone rewards would be $60. You certainly don't want to set yourself back to square one by spending too much here.

Dream about the finish line.

When I was a teenager, I used to keep myself motivated by writing down what I would do with the item I was saving up for. So, every Sunday evening, I would write down what I would do once I bought it, how I would use it, and how it would feel when I used it. Imagining using it and how it will feel reminds you of what you're working toward and why you're saving up. It's easy to forget why you're saving money, which then can easily become a chore. But try to constantly picture yourself achieving that goal. This way, you'll always be reminded why you're giving up your immediate urges to spend and how it will feel to reach your long-term goal.

ACTIVITY

Now that you know how to set goals, put your skill to practice. Set three goals for yourself that you want to achieve financially:

1. Short-term goal (in the next few months or weeks).
2. Mid-term goal (in the next six to twelve months).
3. Long-term goal (anything from one year, three years to five years, depending on how far ahead you want to plan).

Ensure you specify the exact goal (like a specific amount you want to save) and an exact date for each goal. Break these big goals down further and start planning what you have to do each month, week, or day to slowly work toward that goal.

In Chapter 2, we are going to cover a lot of different ways you can start making your own money so that you can reach your goals. Not only will you learn how to make money through side hustles, but you'll also learn how to earn a passive income. There are a lot of possibilities!

2

GETTING YOUR OWN MONEY

Imagine always having your own money and never having to ask your parents for money again! Awesome, right?

To reach your financial goal, you have to earn money to start saving it. But it is a lot easier said than done, especially as a teen. When I was younger, all I wanted was my own money and my own independence. That desire to be independent from my parents sparked many ideas about how to make my own money so that I wouldn't have to ask anybody for anything. Once you have just a small taste of financial independence, you will realize how amazing it is and never look back.

In this chapter, I share many ways you can start generating your own income, both traditionally and nontraditionally. I will cover how to start a side hustle, make money with more traditional approaches, and even how to try making money through passive income. You'll learn about the different ways to earn an income to reach whatever financial goal you have in mind. At first, it might not seem clear or easy, but you just have to know where to start. Keep reading to discover the many different ways you can create income as a teen.

THE BEST WAYS TO ACTIVELY MAKE MONEY AS A TEEN

Getting a Part-Time Job

As simple as it sounds, it's one of the best ways you can make money as a teenager. A part-time job offers you exactly what you need to make money. It tends to be the most consistent and reliable way of earning income, especially if you're working toward a specific goal. And while it might sound like a lot of work and spare time that you lose, having work experience on your resume at a young age will help tremendously in the future. Demonstrating that you aren't afraid to work, even at a young age, will show future employers you're a worthy candidate and improve your chances of landing jobs in the future. It gives you a rock star reputation for being employable right now. Having a consistent part-time job will help you plan your budget better, set higher goals, and help with your overall goal since you can predict what your income will be. Check online for available jobs, or keep an eye out on the local community boards and any vacancies you may hear about. Think about a place you would really like to work part-time and ask about when they might soon be hiring. Plant the seed for a possible part-time job that you will enjoy by giving them your information and letting them know you are interested in working for them. Let's dig deeper.

Doing Odd Jobs

Doing odd jobs for your family or neighbors is a great way to make extra money. You can do this in combination with your part-time job or instead of the part-time job. Odd jobs refer to things you do for other people that aren't necessarily a fixed or predictable source of income. This may include mowing lawns, walking dogs, babysitting, shoveling snow, handiwork, or cleaning services.

Odd jobs are great if you want more time and flexibility and are not ready to commit to the schedule of a part-time job. However, if you're looking to make a fixed amount of money each month, these jobs aren't as reliable. So deciding to take on odd jobs will depend on you, your situation, and what you want to achieve.

You can let your neighbors know you're available to do specific odd jobs by handing out flyers the old-school way. Or consider creating a Facebook post in your local community groups like Front Porch Forum.

Starting Your Own Business

Be your own boss! If you find that these odd jobs are something you're good at and you want to commit more time to them, consider starting your own business. With the technology, resources, and community we have today, teens have more opportunities here than ever before. Think about what you're good at, what interests you, and what you think your community needs.

So, you can either start a business where you promote the physical work you can do, like a dog-walking or babysitting service. Or, you can start a digital business for online work. There is a huge market for web designers, assistants, content creators, and artists. If you're artistic, why not start a business designing book covers and advertisements? If you're good at video editing, why not start a freelance video editing business? Find what you're good at and see how you can use that to start a side hustle for yourself. It may take time in the beginning, and sometimes you have to charge less in the beginning to build up a reputation, but in the long run, it will really pay off!

Having a Yard Sale

We all own a few things we no longer wear or use. And what better way to declutter your life than to find a way to make money out of it? One person's trash is another person's treasure, right? So find a few things you can sell that you no longer use. Also, find out from your parents if they have anything they want to get rid of. You might have to negotiate with them to keep a portion of the money you make for them, but that's extra cash in your pocket.

The yard sale is the most traditional way to display all your unwanted items at once. However, there are many great online places you can advertise it. Many apps and websites allow you to publish your items for people to buy. Vintage goods have never been more popular, so don't be afraid to post just about anything online.

Post your unwanted items online to Front Porch Forums or other sites that don't charge you to advertise items for sale. Using the internet requires very little work. You will be surprised what people will buy and what you can earn by selling the stuff you don't even want anymore.

Investing Money

Investing money in things like stocks, crypto, or mutual funds is something you can start considering—no matter what age you are. These investments are known to grow over time without requiring any work from your side. But it's important to know that these investments are not going to bring you money immediately. These are best for long-term savings and future plans.

One part of your savings plan could be to invest your money as an additional way to save up for your goal. This way, you're not tempted to spend it, and you're also able to increase its value much more than you would with just a simple savings plan. It is super important to do some research about the different investments and speak to someone who has experience in investments and can help you make the right decisions. If your savings goal is something longer term and you have years of savings ahead of you, this is a good option to look at. For those curious to learn more, I will be going into much more detail about investing in Chapter 6.

Selling Items That You Made or Found

Another option to make some money is to sell items you have physically made. This is an excellent option for anyone good at painting, drawing, crafts, or even building furniture. Again, this falls under *starting your own business*, where you should use what you're good at and see how it can make you money.

The other option is to sell physical items that you find, like antiques or collectibles. Thanks to the internet, these collectibles or your own crafts can be sold pretty much anywhere. Research online stores, websites, and communities where you can advertise and sell your goods.

Tutoring

Are you really good at a specific school subject? Why not consider tutoring others who need some help? With all the pressure we experience in schools today, more and more students are turning to tutors for help, and you could be the perfect fit. You can advertise your services at schools with flyers or, again, on social media and among your friends. Don't miss the opportunity to appeal to younger kids as well, like those in elementary school who could do with some help in school.

Speak to Your Parents about Chores

If you're looking for easier ways to make money right at home, why not ask your parents about taking on more chores in the house for some extra money? Discuss anything they need help with that they can let you do for some extra money. There are always opportunities to wash the car, clear the garage, clean the gutters, clean out the pantry, or wash the curtains. These are usually bigger chores your parents don't have time for, which would be perfect for you.

EARNING PASSIVE INCOME AS A TEEN

There are a lot of ways you can make money passively as a teenager; you just have to know where to look!

The examples I have listed above are the most well-known and more traditional ways of making money, where you need to physically do something to receive an income. This is either physically going to work, selling items at a yard sale or online, painting and advertising your work, or actively watching your neighbor's kids. These activities are active ways to make income, but there are other options, too, known as passive income.

Simply put, passive income is money you make automatically and continuously without needing to physically do something more than once. For instance, as a writer, you only write a book once. However, then you make money each time it gets sold without needing to do anything additional. Or, as a YouTuber, you only have to record and upload a video once. Then you're able to make money from it every time someone watches it without needing to do anything again.

Consider things like stock investments that can also be seen as a form of passive income since you invest the money once and don't need to do anything for it to make you more money. Let's take a closer look at a couple of different ways you can make passive income as a teen.

YouTube

As mentioned, YouTube is a fantastic way to make passive income, but it takes a lot of time and commitment at first. And to continue making passive income, it is recommended that you continue uploading videos and growing your account and audience. Even with the amount of time it takes at first to get started, it is a great option for a source of passive income, especially for a teenager. The most popular searches on YouTube are focused on how-to guides and tutorials. So if there is something you're good at that you can teach on your channel, go for it!

Affiliate Marketing

What is affiliate marketing? Affiliate marketing is a wonderful way to make passive income and can be used in combination with a YouTube channel, blog, or just your social media platforms. Affiliate marketing is where you promote a product or a company and get a commission every time someone buys through your recommendation. I'm sure you've seen a few YouTubers mentioning how you can get a special discount by using their link in the description. That is a form of affiliate marketing.

To do this, you don't have to have your own product or buy and resell anything. All you have to do is recommend a certain product, and then you will passively receive money when someone buys it. You can partner with a company whose product you would like to sell and promote on a YouTube channel, a blog, or your social media platforms. Again, like YouTube, you have to invest some time in the beginning to grow your audience and have viewers to whom you can recommend the product. But once you have the following, this becomes a reliable source of passive income.

COMMON QUESTIONS ABOUT PASSIVE INCOME

Passive income can cover a lot of topics and opportunities and also require some things you need to know. It's natural to have some questions about it, and hopefully, some of the answers below will help you.

Can You Live Off of Passive Income?

You can definitely make passive income your entire income, but it may take some time to establish in the beginning. Depending on your chosen route, it may take some initial work to get started, but if you work hard and long enough at it, it can work! Many YouTubers, authors, affiliate marketers, or investors live off of the money they make passively. The most important thing here is to just keep going.

Is Passive Income Worth It?

The thing about passive income is that it may take a lot of time initially, most of which brings no immediate results. So, staying motivated can be extremely tough if you keep working on your channel or book without getting paid for your time right away. But if you finally break through the surface and start making an income, you will see how much value it brings. Because passive income—after it is initially set in place—allows you to continue earning without having to do much, it can be a very attractive kind of income.

ACTIVITY – FIND YOUR INCOME SOURCES

Can you see all the possibilities there are for you to earn some money? Using what you know, make a list of all the things you can do to earn some extra money. Are you good with kids and think you'll be a good babysitter? Or are you extremely creative and ready to start selling your artwork? Are you ready to bust out some odd jobs?

Whatever it is, start by making a list of a few of these methods for making money that you are most drawn to. Don't be afraid to constantly add ideas to that list. The more avenues you try, the better your odds of finding something that will stick.

Once you've got the list, make some notes next to each idea about the next steps to get the ball rolling. So for babysitting or dog-walking services, you might have to start by designing and sharing your advertisement. If you're thinking of making and selling items, your first step would be to gather the materials and start drawing/painting/building.

By writing down these first steps, you're well on your way to getting started. Coming up in Chapter 3, I will be walking you through all the basic details you need to know to create your first budget. Developing and using a budget is where you will start to be able to better manage the money you'll be earning. Not only am I going to show you how to create a basic budget, but I am going to give you some sweet tips and tricks to help you stick to it.

Get psyched! Budgeting is the backbone for reaching your dreams and goals.

3

BUDGETING

A budget is telling your money where to go instead of wondering where it went.

— DAVE RAMSEY

Budgeting should not be intimidating or scary. It can be a helpful tool to change the way you work with money forever. This chapter is all about showing you how simple and effective using a basic budget can be. You will also learn great tips and tricks for maximizing your monthly savings. Budgets are how you become the boss of your money and are truly the backbone for reaching your financial goals and dreams.

THE POINT OF A BUDGET

You will find throughout different aspects of life that you cannot improve on what you don't measure. The only way to truly improve and grow in anything is to find a way and track these improvements. It sounds technical, but it's really simple. Think about weight loss, for instance. How would you know you're improving and losing weight if you didn't know what your starting weight was and what your weight was throughout your journey? The same principle can be used for budgeting and finances. Unless you're measuring your progress somehow, you have no way of telling whether you're making progress.

So, creating a budget can be used as the starting point for your measurements. If you're looking to save a certain amount of money each month or spend less on unnecessary items, you must keep track of your current savings (the money you have now) and the money you're currently spending on unnecessary items (where your money is going). A budget is like the story of the life of your money.

But a budget is so much more than that and has many other benefits.

Here are some more reasons you should consider starting a budget:

- You'll be better prepared for the financial responsibilities of adulthood.

As mentioned before, nobody prepares you for adulthood and all the financial responsibilities that await you. You'll earn large sums of money but also be expected to pay large sums of money. And worst of all, you'll be required to *know* how much to save and spend so that you have enough each month. The best way to prepare for this is by practicing as early as possible and by setting up your budget. By using a budget to track your income, expenses, and savings, you are building a solid foundation for when you are an adult. The concept of a budget won't change—just the amounts and labels will change. So, you'll already know exactly how to keep track of all your money and be better equipped for the future.

- You'll learn how to live within your means and save for things.

One of the biggest challenges many of us face is living within our means and having money left over each month to put into savings. We have so easily fallen into the trap of spending all of our money each month. And sometimes we spend more than we earn, which gets us into debt (owing lots of money to people, banks, and/or credit cards). You don't want to fall into that trap, especially in your youth, and by sticking to a budget, you'll be able to have better control of your money. Your budget will guide you and ensure you stay within the boundaries of what you can afford.

- You'll have a better understanding of money management.

Knowing and understanding money is one of the most powerful skills to have. And your budget will build that foundation for you. Budgets give you a visual idea of money coming into your life and where that money goes. By monitoring and adjusting your budget, you practice a powerful sense of management and control. This understanding of tracking your expenses and your income is an excellent money management skill to have.

- Budgeting helps track your progress.

As you've read at the beginning of this chapter, a budget helps you track your progress and see whether you're on track to reaching your financial goals. Whether you have smaller short-term goals (like buying something specific, like a pair of shoes) or bigger long-term goals (like buying a car), your budget is the key. It is the starting point of all financial progress and success.

- You'll learn about the power of delayed gratification.

It takes real self-control and discipline to say no to something you want right now to save money for something you want in the future. The concept of saying no to something you want right now in exchange for something later is called *delaying instant gratification*. It's something that's hard at first but gets easier the more times you do it. It's similar to saying no to chocolate cake because you know you have a goal of losing 5 pounds. It's really about giving up something you want *now* for something you want the *most*. And if you can do that and give up instant gratification for delayed gratification, you're stronger than many people in society. You'll have a special skill that many people lack. So practice it as often as you can since it is something that will help you tremendously with long-term financial success.

Using a budget is a critical strategy and tool if you want to become a millionaire with a normal job.

HOW TO START A BUDGET AS TEEN

Now that you know *why* you have to start budgeting, let's look at exactly how you can start setting up your first budget. There are some basic steps to take, and from there, you can build it to suit your current situation. These basic guidelines can be used throughout your life for successful budgeting, so let's get right to it!

Calculate Your Income – Money Coming In

The first step to creating a budget is to add up how much money you earn each month. This can be from a single income, like your job. Or, if you have a few different things that provide you with income, you can list them all and total up your earnings. This can be things like an allowance, odd jobs, gifts, etc.

For many teens and adults who don't have a fixed income from a steady job, this amount will change from month to month, which is perfectly fine. You will just need to adjust and monitor your monthly budget and make adjustments if needed.

When adding the amounts to your budget, try listing the different sources of income in their columns, with each amount next to it. Having each income in its own column makes it easier to see exactly where your money comes from and how much you're currently earning from each.

Track Your Expenses – Money Going Out

The next important step in creating your budget is to know what you currently spend. So make a list of everything you spend your money on each month. Track and record every single item you buy, what it is, and how much you spent on it— so that you have a clear picture of your expenses. If you use your bank card, this is easier to track via your bank statements. But using a notebook and pen to track expenses works just as well. Even items you buy in cash should be noted so that you can calculate everything at the end of the month.

Categorize Your Spending

After the first month, look at your list and see what kind of categories these recorded purchases might be grouped into. For instance, if you bought a pair of shoes one day and a jacket the next, you can categorize it all under *Clothes*. Or if you buy food or snacks, all those items can be categorized under *Food or Takeout*. Grouping items by category in your budget will make it easier for you to get an overview of your expenses.

Pinpoint Where You're Spending the Most

When tracking your expenses, you might start to notice there is often a habit or trend of wasteful spending. Wasteful spending is when we fall into a routine of spending money unnecessarily on certain items, often smaller purchases that add up without notice. They subtly eat into our savings without us really noticing.

For some, it's infrequent clothing purchases that aren't necessities. For others, it's takeout on a regular basis. For me, it was a coffee every time I left the house. Maybe it's buying a certain soda or snack every day. Smaller sneaky purchases that add up without us understanding their impact on our savings.

Whatever your guilty pleasure is, pinpoint it and be super aware of it. The more you focus on this, the more you will see how it adds up over time, and you can decide to take action and minimize this spending habit. When your wasteful spending habits aren't flying under the radar any longer, you can save more because you are aware of exactly where you spend money, including the unnecessary or smaller items you buy.

Create Your Budget

Now that you have looked at ways to earn money and tracked your expenses for a month, you will use this information to create a monthly budget. This is where you start taking control and becoming the boss of your money. Building and using a budget is the backbone to reaching your goals, especially bigger goals like buying your first car or becoming a millionaire with a normal job.

As a first-time budget creator, it isn't always clear how it should look, which is why I have created simple templates for you to use. These templates are going to help you look at the story of your money over a period of one month. This will be your monthly budget, and I am going to walk you through each step and make it very easy. Let's get started!

Creating a basic monthly budget consists of four steps:

1. Figuring out your total monthly income.
2. Organizing how much you spend each month by categorizing your spending.
3. Combining these two pieces of information with a plan-ahead strategy to create a basic budget.
4. Maintaining or balancing your budget.

When you unlock the overall picture, you will be empowered to strategize and plan to reach your goals. This is the money map that helps you get where you want to go.

Get excited about learning to use a budget because this is where you start to unlock powerful possibilities!

So grab a piece of paper or get on your computer, and I am going to walk you through how to create and maintain your first monthly budget!

Part One: Figuring out your total monthly income

In this first step, you are going to be organizing all of the ways you make money during the month. Don't worry if your total income doesn't look like a lot of money right now or if you only have one thing listed in the "money coming in" category. The most important and powerful thing here is that you are taking the first step toward creating your first budget. Great job getting started!

1. Recreate the TOTAL MONTHLY INCOME template below on paper or your computer.
2. Write down or fill in each way you plan on earning money monthly in the "category" column.
3. Write down or fill in how much money you earned from each of these categories in the "amount earned" column.
4. Add up all of the amounts in the "amounts earned" column to get your total amount earned or *total monthly income*. Fill in that number in the very bottom right-hand side box.

TOTAL MONTHLY INCOME

Category (WHERE IS THE MONEY COMING FROM?)	Amount Earned (HOW MUCH IS EARNED?)
	$
	$
	$
	$
TOTAL MONTHLY INCOME --->	$

TOTAL MONTHLY INCOME – EXAMPLE

Category	Amount Earned
(WHERE IS THE MONEY COMING FROM?)	(HOW MUCH IS EARNED?)
PART-TIME JOB	$200
BABYSITTING	$30
ALLOWANCE	$40
ADDITIONAL CHORES	$30
TOTAL MONTHLY INCOME --->	**$300**

In this example, the total monthly income is $300.

Part Two: Categorize and determine your total monthly spending

This second step will organize your monthly spending based on the tracking you have done into categories, and then you will add everything up to get your total monthly spending. Just like when you were figuring out your monthly income, if any categories don't match what your day-to-day looks like, change them to what makes sense for you.

1. Recreate the TOTAL MONTHLY SPENDING template below on paper or your computer.
2. Using the information you gathered from tracking your spending, fill in all of the categories for your spending in the "spending category" column.

3. Next, fill in each amount you spent in the "amount spent" column for each of your categories.

4. Finally, total up all of the "amount spent" figures, and you will get your "total amount spent" for the month.

TOTAL MONTHLY SPENDING

Spending Category (What are you buying?)	Amount Spent (How much are you spending?)
CLOTHING	$
FOOD AND DRINKS	$
ART SUPPLIES	$
VIDEO GAMES	$
OTHER	$
TOTAL AMOUNT SPENT --->	$

Here is an example of how this might look:

TOTAL MONTHLY SPENDING – EXAMPLE

Spending Category (What are you buying?)	Amount Spent (How much are you spending?)
CLOTHING	$100
FOOD AND DRINKS	$50
ART SUPPLIES	$60
VIDEO GAMES	$50
OTHER	$40
TOTAL MONTHLY SPENDING --->	$300

Part Three: Creating your monthly budget

In this last step, you will put it all together and create your first monthly budget. You will be looking at your total monthly income, planning your spending ahead of time, as well as *continuing to track how you spend money.* This is what using a budget means, and this is a really big deal. It is what allows you to take control of your money so you can make plans and set goals.

The budget column is where you will plan and decide in advance how much you want to spend for each category. By planning ahead of time, you have created the option to save money each month, unlocking the power to create a savings plan. This is when you truly start taking control of your own money! Adding a "budget" column into the mix is truly the most magical part of this proven money strategy.

After creating your monthly budget, it will need to be updated as you spend money throughout the month. This doesn't take a lot of time, but it is a critical part of using a budget.

Let's get started!

1. Recreate the template below on paper or your computer.
2. Go back and look at part one of this exercise to find your total monthly income and decide how you want to divide it up between each of your spending categories. How much do you plan to spend for each category during the month?
3. Next, fill in those amounts in the "budget" column next to each category.
4. One of the golden rules of using a budget is to *make sure that the total budgeted amount does not exceed your total monthly income.*

MONTHLY BUDGET

Expenses (What are you buying?)	Amount Budgeted (How much would you like to spend?)	Actually Spent (How much did you actually spend?)	Difference (Subtract what you spent from what you budgeted)
CLOTHING	$	$	$
FOOD & DRINKS	$	$	$
ART SUPPLIES	$	$	$
VIDEO GAMES	$	$	$
OHER	$	$	$
Monthly Totals	Income: $	Spent: $	Income minus Spent: $

You have now officially created your first monthly budget and are actively taking control of your money, mostly because you are *planning your spending ahead of time.* This is a REALLY big deal, and you should feel very proud of yourself!

Part Four: Maintaining your budget

Hurray! You have built your first monthly budget! Now what? Maintaining a budget means checking in and updating it at least once a week as you spend money and if your amount earned figure changes. This is also referred to as *balancing your budget.* The good news here is that updating your budget can be very quick and straightforward.

Here are the three simple steps to maintaining your budget:

1. Update your "actually spent" sections as you spend money.
2. Next, update the "difference" section.
3. Finally, update the "monthly total spent" and "difference" in the bottom row.

The Golden Rule: *You never want your monthly spending to exceed your total income.*

If you have spent more than your budgeted amount, put a negative sign next to the difference amount. Be aware if you have overspent so you can make better choices moving forward. Especially as an adult, being able to avoid overspending will help you stay out of debt and avoid being dead broke.

Now, let's look at some example budgets by plugging in some numbers to show you how some different scenarios might look.

EXAMPLE BUDGET #1 – Spending less than your total monthly income

Expenses Categories	Amount Budgeted	Amount Spent	Difference
CLOTHING	$75	-$50	$25
FOOD & DRINKS	$40	-$50	-$10
ART SUPPLIES	$25	-$10	$15
VIDEO GAMES	$20	-$20	$0
OTHER	$40	-$30	$10
Monthly Totals	**Income:** $200	**Spent:** -$160	**Income minus Spent:** $40

Congrats! You spent less than you earned in this example! You have $40 left over for savings!

Now let's look at a second example where the spending has exceeded the total income.

EXAMPLE BUDGET #2 – Spending more than your total monthly income

Expense Categories	Amount Budgeted	Amount Spent	Difference
CLOTHING	$75	-$70	$5
FOOD & DRINKS	$40	-$50	-$10
ART SUPPLIES	$25	-$25	$0
VIDEO GAMES	$20	-$40	-$20
OTHER	$40	-$40	$0
Monthly Totals	**Income:** $200	**Spent:** -$225	**Income minus Spent:** -$20

In this scenario, because you have spent more than you earned —you owe $20 as a debt, and there are no savings.

COMMIT TO STICKING TO YOUR BUDGET

Make a promise to yourself to stick to your budget as much as possible to ensure your goals are reached in the long run. If you only allocated $20 to video games each month, then be aware of when you have reached that amount and avoid spending any more for that category. Try your best to stick to the amounts you planned to spend, or else the budget becomes pointless.

Commit yourself to stick to your budget so that you know exactly how you are spending your hard-earned money. This proven money strategy of using and sticking to a budget will absolutely benefit you in the long run.

COMMON BUDGETING MISTAKES TO AVOID

Making Tracking Hard

The fact that you have to track every single one of your expenses can become very time-consuming, so find a way to make it as easy as possible—whatever that looks like for you. You might prioritize only swiping your debit card so that all your expenses are on your bank statement. Or, you can use an app that links to your account and helps you track it. Recently, I've seen some banks categorize certain purchases based on categories too. Even using a small notebook to keep track of expenses will work. You just need to find the habit and tool that works best for you.

Whatever it is, don't make it hard for yourself by trying a very time-consuming method. Find an easy way that doesn't take a lot of time so it's easier to stick with the tracking.

Expecting It to Always Be the Same

As much as you want it to be, your budget is never going to be the same. Your expenses won't be the same each month, and if you have a job that doesn't have a set schedule or paycheck, your income might also vary. It's important to adjust your budget accordingly each month so that you don't end up over-spending. So if you work less and have less income, adjust your budget accordingly.

You may have to shop less, but at least you'll still be staying on track and ensuring you put money in savings—even if it is less than usual. The thing is, in other months, you may earn more, but that doesn't mean you want to dramatically increase your expenses too. Making more money doesn't mean you should spend more. Either keep that extra money for the months you'll be earning less or save as much as possible.

Not Constantly Revising the Budget

If you've created a budget for yourself for the first time, you might see that there are things that work and things that don't work for you. Perhaps you budgeted way too much for clothes but not enough for your fun activities. Maybe you have more money left over each month and can afford to save more toward your goal. Whatever the case, you will have to revise your budget often and see if there are any changes you can make. It can be a monthly revision or a bimonthly. It's really up to you and your circumstances. But don't just leave your budget alone without checking whether it's still working for you and helping you succeed.

Not Budgeting for Fun Things Too

When creating a budget, it is very easy to be hard on ourselves and force ourselves to save almost all our money without leaving some opportunity to enjoy the moment. While saving is important, you are still young and should enjoy the moments you have in your youth. So yes, be driven and put money away toward your savings. But also allow yourself to spend some money on yourself and fun activities with your friends. It's about the balance.

ACTIVITY

With the template idea above, create your own budget. Add the items that suit your situation and fill in the amounts to the best of your abilities. From here, you can also start tracking your expenses, which will give you a clearer, more detailed view of the amounts in your budget. This activity may take a month or two to get the correct amounts but start today by adding the categories and amounts you already know.

With the help of your budget, the next chapter will show you all the different ways you can cut down your expenses and save money without having to make huge changes.

4

SAVING MONEY

Save money, and money will save you!

Money is something we cannot avoid, and it is often one of the biggest stressors in people's lives. Between worrying about bills, thinking about savings, planning for the future, and having enough money, it can quickly become overwhelming. One of the best ways to reduce the stress money can cause is to start saving it. This chapter is focused on simple tips and tricks you can use to save money easily and without even noticing it.

WHY YOU SHOULD START SAVING MONEY AS A TEEN

Having a savings account that continuously grows is incredibly powerful and will benefit you greatly. The practice of saving money has many benefits, so take the opportunity to create good things for yourself by developing this money strategy. The earlier you start saving, the better your finances will be, and the more likely you'll be to thrive financially in the future and reach your goals

As Chapter 2 explained, there are so many ways you can start earning money as a teenager, and your greatest advantage is to start building your savings when you are younger. Of course, the money you earn can also be used for your day-to-day, but the focus should be on saving as much as you possibly can, as soon as you can.

When I was a teenager, I didn't really understand why saving was important, and I almost immediately spent all the money I earned. I was convinced I was still young and meant to enjoy my teens. I thought I would be able to save money easily as an adult since I would be earning bucketloads of money, and it would be easier to save up. What I didn't consider is that while my income was a lot higher as an adult, my expenses were a lot higher too. So the decision to save money or not should never be dependent on how much money you are making. No matter how much money you are making, if you don't have a savings plan, it is super easy to find lots of things to spend money on and spend it all quickly. However, if you make saving a priority and have a plan, you'll reap the benefits for decades.

Here's what I mean:

- **Savings Helps for Emergencies**

The number of times my savings have helped me out of some really tricky situations cannot be emphasized enough. Even as a young teen, there may be emergencies that you'll face where some money is required. This could be anything from car repairs to medical bills or a new phone in case of damage. Having some money saved up for the unexpected is always a good idea. It can be kept separate from your other savings so that your emergency funds only ever get used for unpredictable situations.

- **Savings Allows for More Fun in Your 20s**

Let's face it, you know your twenties are going to be filled with fun, adventure, and exploration, and you want to be prepared for that. So by starting your savings plan as a teenager, you'll be sure to have money for new activities, traveling, or college. Depending on what you're planning, this savings account can be extremely useful if you decide to take a trip abroad or move to a new state. Don't underestimate the power of the money you start saving today for big things in a few years.

- **Savings Builds Self-Reliance**

The older we get, the less our parents tend to buy for us, and that can become challenging if you have no way of paying for your own things. If you start saving money early on while still living with your parents, you can ensure you have money and be reliant when moving out of the house. There is no greater feeling than being independent. Living off your own money is the most significant sign of independence. Our parents can't look after us forever. By saving from an early age, we're preparing ourselves for when they stop paying for our expenses.

- **Savings Helps Achieve Big Goals Sooner**

Future purchases like a car or a house can be pretty expensive and take years of planning, savings, and loans. But it doesn't have to take that long if you just plan for it from an early age. If you have savings to back you up, you can put down a down payment on these items which will lessen the time period that you have to pay for these items. You can cut down how long you pay for a house or a car by *several years* if you just make a large enough down payment. By paying off a car or house sooner, you'll have financial freedom at a younger age than most while having an incredible asset in your possession. It sets you ahead in life, and all you have to do is simply put some money away each month as a teenager.

- **Savings Helps You Avoid Credit**

While it is important to build up your credit score to qualify for things like houses or cars, it is important not to rely on credit cards for these really big purchases. Essentially, because credit cards and loans often carry expensive interest rates, you end up paying much more than the original price. It's so easy to apply for credit cards and have a "buy now, pay later" mentality. But this mentality can quickly spiral out of control and set you back *years*. If you have a savings account and find yourself in a situation where you need some extra help, you can use money from your savings instead of depending on your credit card and paying unnecessary interest. Not even sure what a credit score is? Don't worry; we will be discussing all of the basics of credit usage you need to know in Chapter 7.

HOW TO SAVE MONEY AS A TEEN

Understanding the importance of a savings plan is one thing, but knowing how to get started is another. It isn't always clear, and knowing where to start can sometimes be challenging. This is one reason that teens often do not take the time to learn about finances and the power of saving. So if you're ready to start saving money, good for you for getting this far!

For the best results, here is a simple process for saving money you should try:

- **Start with a plan and plan ahead**

Budgeting was a great first step to starting a savings plan since you can see what you earn vs. what you spend and plan your spending ahead of time. This gives you a great indication of where your money goes and where you can reduce expenses. Looking at your expenses, start determining what you want, what you need, and what you can live without. If you separate your expenses that way, you'll be able to cut out the things you can live without and use that money for your savings instead.

Now, when you're on the verge of buying something, take a second to think to yourself, "Do I need this? Do I want this?" Or "Can this money be better spent in the future?" By starting this habit, you will start to understand how many times you spent money in the past without giving it much thought. When you don't give your purchases much thought, you spend your hard-earned money quickly, often leaving you with nothing to show for it in the long run.

Using a plan and planning your spending ahead of time allows you to decide beforehand what purchases are necessities, luxuries, and nonessentials. Have a look at your bank statement or the items you tracked on your spending tracker. You can plan these items for the future and decide which items you won't be buying again. You are taking control and planning ahead, which is really powerful stuff.

- **Open a savings account**

Good news! It is easy to open a bank account that includes a savings account, although you might need some assistance from your parents or guardians. Luckily, it is a quick and simple process. After you have set up your bank account, you can have a fixed amount of money automatically transferred into the savings section. By doing this, you'll never see the money in your savings account, making it easy not to miss it.

After you are comfortable using the basic set up of your account, you should try to save using more than one savings account, so you can separate it into categories like emergency funds, short-term savings, and long-term savings. A common goal to shoot for is to save 10% of your income, whether you have a job or are dependent on your allowance. This 10% can either go into one savings account each month, or you can split it, so a little is separated into each savings account.

If you can, you should also think about setting up the accounts so that you aren't able to access that money until a set date. This makes it easier to force yourself to stick to the savings plan and not withdraw the money unnecessarily. These dates can be set for a few months or a few years, and you would need the bank's permission to use that money before that time.

An even easier alternative to using a bank to start saving money is to use an app specifically geared toward kids and teenagers such as Greenlight. This app is from a financial technology company and not a bank, but it still has features for saving, investing, and monitoring your savings. There is a link to learn more about Greenlight in the resources section at the end of this book.

It is not important which tool you end up using to start saving. What matters is getting a savings plan started as soon as possible.

- **Earning money with savings account interest**

As you begin researching different banks and saving accounts and deciding where to keep your money, you will hear the term "interest rate." An interest rate for a savings account is *the amount of money banks will pay you just for keeping your money in these accounts.* Yes, you will earn money just by keeping your money in the bank. The amount of interest you earn is based on a percentage of how much money you have in your account. In other words, the amount in your account multiplied by the interest rate percentage gives you the amount you will earn just for keeping your money there.

There are two basic types of interest rates: simple interest and compound interest.

1. Simple interest is calculated by using your initial investment amount times the interest rate. This calculation doesn't change and uses the same initial deposit amount every year to calculate the interest you earn.

2. Compound interest is different because it calculates the interest you earn using your initial amount invested PLUS any previously earned money from interest. In other words, it uses whatever your new total amount is every year and multiplies that by the interest rate to calculate your yearly earnings. With compound interest, when the total amount in your savings account increases, the amount of interest you earn also

increases. Using compound interest, you can earn even faster.

Let's look at these two interest rate types through an example using a $1,000 initial deposit invested with both simple and compound interest rates of 3%.

Simple interest

With a simple interest rate of 3% and $1,000 in your account, you will earn $30 (3% of $1,000) every year just for keeping your money there. Even if you deposit more money into the account, the initial $1,000 amount is what is used annually to calculate the interest earned.

Compound interest

With a compound interest rate of 3% annually and a $1,000 initial deposit in your account, you will earn $30 (3% of $1,000) the first year and have a new balance amount of $1,030.

However, in the second year, you will earn that 3% *on the new higher total amount.* Let's say during the second year, you have also managed to deposit $400 additional savings into your savings account, bringing your total balance to $1,430 ($400 additional savings plus the $1,030 balance from the previous year). Using compound interest, in the second year, you will earn $43 (3% of $1,430). You earn interest on your new higher totals and make even more money.

Now, let's say during the third year, you manage to deposit $600 more into your savings account, and your new balance is

$2,030. With a 3% compound interest rate, you will earn $61 (3% of $2,030).

You can start to see that compound interest is a pretty big deal and a huge opportunity to take advantage of, especially if you are starting young. This is why I have devoted the entire next chapter to exploring the topic in more detail.

- **Start small**

The biggest misconception about saving money is that you have to do it all the time. But that's the best thing about saving—that it just takes a small amount consistently to make a big impact. It's better to save a few dollars each month than to occasionally put money away. The key is to start with what you can afford, and again, that's something you'll know by creating and using a budget. Every little bit you put away eventually adds up and snowballs into larger amounts over time. So, even if you just save a few dollars every week, that's fantastic! You'll be better off than not saving anything at all.

We often fall into a mindset of *all or nothing*, where you think that if you're not saving hundreds, it doesn't make a difference. But it's time to change that mindset and start reminding yourself that something is better than nothing and consistency is really the key to success.

- **Invest in yourself**

One of the best investments you can ever make in life is the investment in yourself. This means continuing to put energy into educating, growing, and improving yourself, your skills, and your knowledge. Remember that while possessions and other assets in the world can come and go, the knowledge that you build up cannot be taken from you. So invest in educational books, experiences, seminars, and courses—anything that can help you grow as a person. For example, you are investing in yourself right now by choosing to read this book so you can develop your money knowledge and strategies. Well done!

On a physical level, it is really important to implement this "investment mindset" as well. Investing in your emotional and physical health is super beneficial and important because it impacts everything in your day-to-day life. So invest in good nutrition, hobbies, some form of exercise, and anything that will help your mental health. By investing in maintaining good health, you will save yourself tons of money down the line and avoid the need to treat illness and disease because you neglected your health.

- **Save for the future**

When starting this chapter, I discussed the importance of saving for future things, like traveling in your twenties or buying a house later on in life. This is something I will often repeat because I want you to understand how important it is to just start considering this bigger picture today—right now, in fact. Because the earlier you start saving, the better off you will be and the more amazing and less stressful your life can be. Just starting with the smallest amount will make a big difference down the road, especially since you have the advantage of starting young and if you put the money into accounts that have great compound interest rates.

- **Live below your means**

Living below your means simply means that you should spend less than what you make. This sounds logical since you can't spend what you don't have. But that's how people start getting into credit card debt and spending more than they make. You can enforce living below your means by cutting out unnecessary costs and finding areas where you can reduce spending.

By dividing your expenses into three categories: what you need, what you want, and what you can't live without, you're already one step closer to cutting down on your expenses. You can make it even simpler and more powerful by dividing your expenses into two categories: *needs* and *wants*. Anything that simply falls into the "want" category, you now have the opportunity to start eliminating those expenses that don't really serve you in the long run.

And guess what? Chances are you won't miss a lot of them either. If it isn't something you need, ask yourself whether it is worth your hard-earned money. Is it really worth the hours you spent earning that money? Or will the money be better off in a savings account, serving you for years to come? In most cases, you will see you can save a lot of money by not making small purchases of unnecessary items.

- **Save your change**

One of the very easiest ways to save money is to save your change. If you work with cash often, you can start a savings plan by saving all your physical change in a piggybank, a big jar with a narrow top, or somewhere else you can't easily access the money. Whenever you have change lying around, put it into a savings container instead of spending it. This is a great example of *something being better than nothing*. As you keep putting away a nickel or a dollar or two, you will be surprised to see how quickly those seemingly small amounts add up over time.

- **Shop around for deals**

If you're going to be spending money, make sure you at least spend your money wisely by taking some time to seek out deals and promotions. Instead of buying the first thing you see or from the first store you find, look around and find deals. There is never just one store selling a product, and there is a chance that other stores might be selling the same item for less. Sometimes a store has a flash sale or simply sells the product for less. So, remember to invest some extra time in finding good deals where you will automatically be saving money with each purchase.

This goes for coupons and vouchers as well, which will help significantly with saving money. With big companies constantly competing for your attention, coupons and discounts are more accessible than ever—so make use of them!

If you are a student, some places also offer a discount since you're younger. So have a look at stores that offer discounts for students. Once you start looking for deals, you won't believe how much money you can save with each purchase.

- **Make it at home**

How often are you spending money on items you could have easily made at home? It is so easy to fall into the trap of convenience, where you would rather pay someone else to do it than do it yourself. So, we buy convenient meals, coffees, or even water while we're on the go. With time, these small amounts add up, and we spend a lot more than we think. So if you know that you tend to buy convenient lunches or coffees, try to plan your day so that you prepare them at home instead. You will save yourself so much money in the long run. Look at it this way. If you're buying a simple sandwich five days a week at Subway for $5, it doesn't necessarily feel like you're spending that much a week.

But what you don't consider is that it adds up to $25 a week, $100 a month, and a whopping $1,200 a year! If you made a sandwich at home and didn't buy those sandwiches, you could invest $1,200 every year and earn interest on it too! From the age of sixteen until you graduate, that's an incredible $3,600 (without interest) just by not buying a sandwich. Think about the compound interest money you could make off of $3,600 too!

ACTIVITY

Use what you've learned in this chapter to find ways to save money. Create a list of ways you think you'll be able to save money. Do you use cash frequently, allowing you to save your change? Or are you going to be more conscious of your small purchases and actively stop partaking in them? By creating a list you can constantly check, you'll be more inclined to stick with it.

Congratulations! You've already done tremendous work so far learning how to set goals, create budgets, make money, and save money. In the next chapter, I will teach you more about the power and strategy of using compound interest and how easy it is to make extra money on top of your savings—just by knowing where to keep it.

5

COMPOUND INTEREST

How teens can become millionaires with normal jobs!

In the previous chapter, I briefly touched on the basic idea of interest, but you need an entire chapter to highlight how powerful it can be. In school, the idea of interest and compound interest has probably been talked about, but so briefly that it never stuck with you. Believe me, it never stuck with me either. But when I started learning more about it, and how powerful it can be financially, I never looked at money, savings, or interest the same way again. Using compound interest is your biggest advantage and most powerful tool to becoming a millionaire with a normal job.

Compound interest is a way of multiplying your money, so if there is one chapter that should stick with you, it's this one. Knowing how to calculate compound interest is what drove me to take action and start saving, and I hope it can do the same for you. If you've ever dreamed about the millionaire lifestyle but couldn't do it with a normal job, understanding compound interest is the first step.

WHAT IS COMPOUND INTEREST?

The simple explanation of compound interest is that it makes you more money as your money grows. The reason compound interest is often considered the "8th wonder of the world" is because of how it multiplies amounts quickly and steadily which is fantastic when we are talking about amounts of money.

The problem is that not enough people make an effort to save money and benefit from compound interest. The younger you are, the sooner you can start compounding, and the more money it will become. Do you now see why it is so important to start saving as early as possible?

Even better is that compound interest requires no actual work to make the money. It just requires you to leave the interest alone and allow the savings to continue growing. Of course, you can keep adding money to the savings account so that the amount grows (which means more interest). It is a really good strategy to try and add money to these savings accounts as often as possible to stimulate more growth and a bigger amount earned from interest.

Taking full advantage of compound interest is one of the most important strategies to becoming a millionaire with a normal job.

HOW COMPOUND INTEREST WORKS

Scenario one:

Let's look again at another real-life example of basic compound interest.

You initially invest $1,000 and will be earning a 5% compounding interest rate each year.

After the first year, you earn 5% on $1,000, which is $50 and brings your account to a total of $1,050.

After the second year, you earn 5% on $1,050, which is $52.50, and brings your account to a total of $1102.50.

In this example, you are never adding any extra money to the account. Your balance   continues to grow year-over-year by earning interest on your original amount plus the interest from the previous years.

Let's continue this example for an even longer period to truly show you the power of compound interest:

Total for year 1: $1,000 + $50 earned interest = **$1,050**
Total for year 2: $1,050 + $52.50 earned interest = **$1,102.50**
Total for year 3: $1,102.50 + $55.12 earned interest = **$1,157.63**
Total for year 4: $1,157.63 + $57.88 earned interest = **$1,215.51**
Total for year 5: $1,215.51 + $60.77 earned interest = **$1,276.28**

Total for year 10: $1,628.89
Total for year 15: $22,078.93
Total for year 20: $2,653.73

Scenario two:

Now let's look at how much more you will earn from the same 5% compound interest if you make additional deposits into your savings account every year to add to the total.

If you make the same initial deposit of $1,000 into your account with the same 5% compound interest rate—but this time, starting in the second year, you deposit $500 of additional savings into your account every year. This is what it would look like over the same 20-year period:

Total for year 1: $1,000 + $50 earned interest = **$1,050**
($1,050 + $500 = $1,550)
Total for year 2: $1,550 + $77.50 earned interest = **$1,627.50**
($1,627 + $500 = $2,127)
Total for year 3: $2,127 + $106.35 earned interest = **$2,233.88**
($2,233.88 + $500 = $2,733.88)
Total for year 4: $2,733.88 + $136.69 earned interest = **$2,869.66**
($2,869.66 + $500 = $3,369.66)
Total for year 5: $3,369.66 + $168.48 earned interest = **$3,538.14**
Total for year 10: $7,278
Total for year 15: $12,052

Total for year 20: $ 18,145

Whoa! You can see what a big difference there is between these two scenarios using compound interest.

After 20 years of 5% compound interest:

Without any additional deposit, your total is **$2,653.**

With the additional yearly deposit of just $500, your total is **$18,145.**

COMPOUND INTEREST COMPARED TO SIMPLE INTEREST

To really highlight the power of compound interest, I am going to compare the same scenario as the two above using simple interest. This should really drive home the point of why compound interest is amazing and powerful and that you should start taking advantage of it as soon as possible.

Remember, with compound interest, you earn interest on the total amount of your investment, which is the original amount plus any interest earned and additional deposits. With simple interest, *you only earn interest on the amount of money you originally invested.*

With your initial original investment of $1,000 and earning 5% simple interest, this is what it would look like over the same 20-year period:

Total for year 1: $1,000 original + 5% on $1,000 = **$1,050**

Total for year 2: $1,050 + 5% on $1,000 = **$1,100**

Total for year 3: $1,100 + 5% on $1,000 = **$1,150**

Total for year 5: $1,250

Total for year 10: $1,500

Total for year 15: $1,750

Total for year 20: $2,000

Do you see how significantly the amounts differ when you compare what you would have earned with compound interest? And compared to compound interest with additional deposits throughout the year?

After 20 years of 5% simple interest, your total is only $2,000. Compare this to the compound interest scenario totals of $2,653 (no additional deposit) and $18,145 (with an additional $500 deposit).

Now you can see the big difference between simple interest, compound interest, and compound interest with additional deposits. Whatever you do in the future, no matter the investment options you take or the savings account you open, always ensure it compounds. Simple interest rarely benefits you, so always aim for accounts that offer compound interest.

ACTIVITY

So far in this chapter, we have looked at examples of simple interest, compound interest, and compound interest with yearly additional deposits to highlight how much more you earn from compound interest. All of this has relied on a lot of math which can seem overwhelming and a bit demotivating. Not everyone loves or is good at math.

Good news! I am now going to share with you a really fantastic website that has a nifty tool that does all of this math for you. It calculates compound interest for you, so now *no math is required on your end*! It figures it all out for you!

This calculator tool allows you to play around with different scenarios like the initial amount deposited, additional deposits, when the interest is calculated, different timespans, and the percentage of the interest rate.

So take a minute to check out this calculator and try out different scenarios to see what magic is possible with compound interest. You will be amazed. Here is the link:

www.nerdwallet.com/banking/calculator/compound-interest-calculator?trk=nw_gn_5.0

HOW TO MAKE COMPOUND INTEREST WORK FOR YOU

The sooner you start saving money, the more time you have to make your money grow. This is why saving early is so important. Even the smallest amount of money you can afford to put away each month will add tremendously to the long-term gain, especially with compound interest and starting at a young age.

The key thing to remember is that you should reinvest the interest you have earned back into your investment to allow for a great accumulation of money. If you withdraw the interest you earned, you will start from square one every time. You have to leave the money in the account so that your money can work for you instead of you having to work for it. This idea of reinvesting your interest is known as "compounding your gains" and is a powerful way to accelerate your wealth-building efforts.

There are some extraordinarily powerful stories of teens who have used the power of compound interest to build themselves immense wealth. The earlier you start, the more money you can make with the least amount of effort. Let's look at an example of how the earlier you start, the better off you are.

A girl I went to college with explained to me how she'd been saving up with compound interest for *years*. This concept sounded crazy to me, but little did I know I'd be writing a book around this topic. Her parents helped her save money for her fourteenth birthday and explained how compound interest worked. She worked part-time jobs throughout high school and put every single penny into this savings account. We stayed in touch for years after college. Five years after graduating college, I found out she could put down a cash deposit for her house using the money she made through her compound savings account. At that stage, I could barely make rent each month. Compound interest truly works. Let's investigate how:

If you start saving $100 a month at the age of 15 and stop at the age of 30, you will have a total of about $18,100. This may not seem like a lot, but remember that all changes when compound interest comes into play, as you will continue earning on top of this, even if you stop adding money to the investment. If you invested that same $100 every month into an account with compound interest at 5%, you would have $26,690 by the time you turned 30 and $196,892 by the age of 60!

THE THREE RULES OF COMPOUND INTEREST

Hopefully, you now understand the power of compound interest. There are three key things to always remember that will ensure nothing but success on your investment journey.

- **Start investing early:**

As you can see from the examples above, the real power lies in starting early. Your investments will start to double as the compound interest increases. In the beginning, the interest may be little and the growth slow, but the snowball effect is real, and you'll watch your money double.

- **Don't take any money out of the investment:**

Tying in with the first point, you don't ever want to remove any money from the investment, or you'll jeopardize the entire system. Your growth will decrease rapidly, and you'll put a complete stop to your snowball.

- **Keep adding to the investment:**

Of course, your money will grow by itself without your help. But if you want to speed up the process and increase the total amount you'll have, you should add as often as you can. The more you add, the greater the amount you'll gain interest in, and the quicker your snowball with gain momentum.

WHERE YOU'RE MOST LIKELY TO EXPERIENCE COMPOUND INTEREST

It is worth taking some time here to understand the best options when it comes to taking advantage of the compound effect.

Savings Accounts & Checking Accounts

When opening a savings account at a bank, chances are there will be both savings and checking options for you to choose from. Both of these generally offer the compounding effect that will build your interest based on your original investment and the interest you already earned. But be sure to ask specifically about this detail and the percentage rate they offer. As a safe option and a starting point for saving money, a bank account is a great choice.

401 or Other Retirement Investments

If you're thinking of retirement plans already (don't worry—I'll be giving you an overview on this topic later on in the book), a 401 account is a great option especially because the interest they add is compounded as well. As with all other compound savings plans, the more frequently you add, the more your money adds up, and the greater your amount of money will be by the time you retire. If you're curious to learn more about that, you will find a complete breakdown of retirement planning in Chapter 11.

Credit Cards

While compound interest can really work in our favor, it can also work against us, especially in the case of credit cards. In Chapter 7, you will learn all about credit cards and how useful they can be *when used correctly*. But when they aren't used responsibly, they can create a mountain of problems for us. With irresponsible credit card habits, there are certain circumstances in which the compound effect will magnify what you owe.

When you fall behind with your payments, it's not about simply paying the money when you have it. Credit cards also take advantage of the compound effect, as well as the fees, which will compound your debt. Before you know it, you can end up paying significantly more than if you just saved up to buy the item with your own money. The good news is that this book is going to show you how to avoid getting into those situations in the first place.

ACTIVITY

Congratulations, potential millionaires! You are just about halfway through the book and have learned some seriously powerful and essential financial basics. You should be very proud of yourself. The topics and strategies we have covered so far, if applied, are going to set you up for having a great foundation for a fantastic life.

Your activity here is to do something nice for yourself—to celebrate yourself for having the motivation and initiative to get this far. This is a reward milestone!

In the next chapter, you will learn about investing, how it works, and why it's an important step to building wealth. We will also dispel some common myths about investing and cover basic investment opportunities.

MAKE SURE YOU'RE NOT THE ONLY ONE WITH MONEY!

Picture this scenario: You've saved diligently, putting your budgeting skills to good use and making every cent count. You've had a clear goal from the beginning: to save for the vacation of a lifetime.

You're ready to pick your destination and rally your friends... and then you realize that not one of them has managed to save as much as you have.

As you employ the skills you're picking up in this book, your financial skills will far outweigh those of most of your peers. And while you're the one in the better position, life would be even better if your friends had the money skills you do.

It's my goal to teach these skills to as many teenagers as I can... and the more people I can reach, the more young people will be able to save for those special goals.

You can help me to do that... and it won't take more than a few minutes of your time.

By leaving a review of this book on Amazon, you'll show other teens and young people where they can find the financial guidance schools fail to teach, and more people will discover these essential skills.

Simply by letting other readers know how this book has helped you and what they can expect from it, you'll guide them toward the important lessons they'll never get in school.

With a bit of luck, some of those readers will be your friends... and you'll have vacation buddies when you finally meet that savings goal!

Thank you for your support. All young people deserve to have this knowledge, and it's my mission to make sure they do.

6

INVESTING

 You cannot save time for future use. But you can invest it for the future you.

— ANONYMOUS

You've learned all the basics of budgeting, earning, and saving, and now you will be introduced to investments. In this chapter, you will learn exactly how it works, why it's important for financial success, and what common myths you should forget. Anyone can get started, teens included, and it's truly one of the best ways to get on the path to becoming a millionaire with a normal job. Investing is like the money garden that multiplies and grows as you sleep.

So what is investing?

Now that you understand how compound interest works, you will better understand the concept of investing. Essentially, investing is another strategy of putting your money somewhere and expecting it to grow and multiply. There are many different avenues and types of investments available. We will cover some of these in this chapter to help you understand the overall concept of investing.

Again, investing means you put your money somewhere with the belief that it will grow. Some people invest using lots of analysis to understand how those investments work, while others invest money in places based on what others recommend. As you start, it is best to use what others recommend. Then as you watch your investment, you will better understand the investment world and can invest money based on your own increased understanding. People invest money because they have the opportunity to make more money and don't have to do much work. And just like compound interest, the more you add, the more you can make.

HOW INVESTMENTS WORK

Different types of investments are available, and you can choose an investment based on what you prefer and what best suits your budget. We'll explore those investments in the next section. To start understanding the basics, let's use the example of buying stocks. Most of you have probably heard of the stock market and understand it is tied to investing money in some way. But how does it work?

At the most basic level, when you invest in stocks, it essentially means you're buying a piece of the company. When the company grows and makes money, the value of the company increases, and therefore so does your "stock" or piece of owner-ship. When you eventually want to sell your stock, you can cash out and make a profit in the process—if when you decide to sell, it is worth more than what you bought it for. Of course, this depends on whether the company's value has increased with time.

A great example of this is the company Apple. In 2007, you could buy a single share of Apple stock for $6. If you had bought 10 shares, you would have paid $60. By 2022, Apple's shares were valued at $148 per share, meaning the stock you bought in 2007 for $60 would now be worth $1,480. If you sold your shares, you would make a $1,420 profit. Pretty straight-forward, right?

Here's the twist. A really important thing to remember about any type of investment is that it isn't a straight line. All invest-ments go up and down in value over time, meaning your stock increases and decreases in value. Sometimes these are steep inclines or declines. In other cases, they increase or decrease by only a few cents. The key is to stay cool-headed and make rational decisions about when to sell your stock. Investing in stocks does involve a level of risk because of their constant increase and decrease in value.

In the long run, investments generally increase in value as the economy grows, so it's a great type of investment for long-term growth and wealth building.

TYPES OF INVESTMENTS FOR TEENS

Here is an overview of some of the available options, so you can start looking at the ones that might interest you the most.

529 College Savings Plan

The college savings plan is exactly what it says it is—it's a way of saving for your degree from early on. One of the best ways to invest in yourself and your future is to save for college as early as possible.

These 529 plans are different from conventional savings plans. They are a tax-advantaged savings account that will help cover your qualification expenses, including tuition, room, and board. The money in these plans grows tax-deferred, meaning the withdrawals are tax-free as long as they're used for education expenses.

So if you set a goal to save up for college, this is an excellent option since you'll be saving huge sums of money by not paying taxes.

Custodial Account

If you're younger than 18, a custodial account is also a great option, but you may need the help of your parents or guardians. It's an account set up by an adult for a minor (those under 18 years old) with fewer rules or fees. While some accounts require maintaining a minimum balance or withdrawal fees, these types of accounts generally don't. With these accounts, you can start investing in things like stocks or taking out insurance policies, despite being young. It's a great place to get started on any serious investment.

Roth IRA

Roth IRA is another excellent investment if you're thinking long term. It is a retirement account that allows you to contribute after-tax dollars up to a certain amount. That means that all the money invested in these accounts has already been taxed. So when you withdraw the money in your retirement, it is 100% profit, and you will not be taxed on that money in the future. These investments also grow tax-free, and the withdrawals are also free of tax as long as you meet certain requirements.

Stock Market Index Fund

The stock market index fund is essentially where you buy and sell shares of businesses, as with the Apple example. There is a lot of information available to help you choose the right shares, as well as a lot of information on what the share is expected to do. So using all the available information, you can make informed decisions and maximize your investments. There are some great links to specific resources for getting started in the Resource section at the end of this book.

To minimize risk, one of the most important things to remember is that it's best not to put all your eggs in one basket. This means you should try not to invest all of your money in one company. By having your investments in different shares, you don't risk losing all of your investment if the value drops. For example, an ETF or exchange-traded fund is a strategy where different types of investments are placed as a bundle. This is a great way to invest money in different places so that all your eggs aren't in one basket. As an investor, you will buy a basket of investments, and it will include everything from stocks to commodities, Bitcoin, and bonds.

High-Yield Savings Account

A high-yield savings account is an excellent option if you're not ready to invest in things like stocks. It's essentially a savings plan that offers higher interest rates than traditional savings accounts. Remember, interest rates are essentially a percentage of your money that the bank pays you just for storing it there. The more money you deposit, the more you will earn. This is where the power of compound interest comes into play. These savings accounts accumulate compound interest if you leave the money in the account.

If you're not sure what you want to do with your savings or for how long you want to save up, these savings accounts are really the best place to start. They are less risky than investments but often don't offer the same high return as investments. So while you do research on investments and how they work, this is a good place to start putting your money right away.

Real Estate Investment

Real estate is another great investment opportunity, and you shouldn't feel limited because of your age. Real estate is a great way to build wealth over time and is something you can call your own. Investing in real estate means buying a piece of property that you can rent for monthly profits or sell for a once-off profit. This can either be done with living areas, like apartments, or businesses, like office spaces.

Investing in Emergency Funds

In Chapter 4, we've covered the concept of an emergency fund and why it's important. But it's vital that you truly realize how important these funds can be. Having an emergency fund separate from your investments can help tremendously with car repairs and unforeseen medical expenses. I used to say, "It will never happen to me," and I never bothered with an emergency fund. And in my early twenties, a part of my car's engine needed to be replaced, which cost me hundreds of dollars. Having an emergency fund prepares you for these unexpected payments, and it won't force you to spend the money you need that month. Having money saved for emergencies before they happen means you have one less major thing to worry about when they do happen.

Self-Investment

As mentioned before, one of the most important investments you can make is in yourself. Whether investing in your future education or taking the time to do courses and workshops, it's always the best investment. By educating yourself and investing in growth, you're setting yourself up for a lifetime of success. Invest in learning new skills, even if it means taking free online courses (which there are tons of).

The fact that you're reading this book and learning about finances is proof that you're motivated to start investing in yourself. Keep going!

You're never too young to invest, and there are truly many excellent options available to you. However, it is always best to ask for some advice from parents or guardians regarding what to invest in. If your parents aren't sure themselves, first make sure you do speak to someone who knows about investments and can guide you as you start.

TOOLS FOR YOUNG INVESTORS

Apps and Websites

If you're serious about taking action and getting started, you will want to begin by doing a little homework. Good news! There are some great resources and apps designed specifically to help you do your research and make it easier. It's very common for investors to track their finances and investments using an app or website. Some are even specifically designed to help teenagers get started with investments. You will find a list of some resources at the end of the book to help you get started. Remember, as you start, be sure to check the rules and terms. Many accounts require maintaining a minimum invest-ment, while others have monthly fees. So before choosing, compare all of the different options, pricing, and requirements, and if possible, get some external advice from investors who already use these apps.

INVESTING MISTAKES TO AVOID

As first-time investors, it is easy to make a mistake and lose your investment and motivation to try again. Unfortunately, mistakes happen. But, there are certain mistakes you can avoid making that might just help you succeed in the world of investing.

Using Personal Knowledge to Choose Investments

When you're investing in a company, the decision to invest should be based on the numbers. Too many first-time investors base their decision on whether they personally like the company or not. If you're an Android lover, don't let that dictate whether you invest in Apple or not. Don't let your personal feelings get involved with your investments. Use the numbers and statistics to guide you.

Focusing on the Short Term

This is a common mistake you will constantly read about and worth mentioning a few times. Don't invest with a focus on the short term. Don't invest with the hopes of making huge profits within a few months. And most importantly, don't judge the value of an investment solely based on what happened in a few months. The company is bound to go up and down in value over the course of a few months. If you track it month by month, you will be frightened by what you see. Remember, all investments are long-term focused, and the growth will only really be clear after a few years. Be patient, and don't withdraw your money if the short-term results aren't what you expect.

ACTIVITY

If you're excited about the idea of investing, you will just increase this excitement by doing some research. So get started by doing some research and find one or two types of investments you find interesting. Learn how they work and what would be expected from you. Doing your research is the first step in succeeding with investments, and make sure that the investments you choose align with your goals and timelines.

At the end of the book, you can find some great resources for getting started doing your homework for your first investment.

While investments are one of the most important aspects of building long-term wealth, they aren't the only thing to focus on. In the next chapter, we'll discuss credit cards and credit scores and how they play into ensuring you continuously and successfully build wealth.

7

USING CREDIT

Y ou've probably heard about credit cards and have some idea of the pros and cons that come with them. In this chapter, we'll discuss credit and credit cards in depth and how to use them responsibly. They can be exceptionally useful, but only when used correctly. They can also cause lots of trouble if used irresponsibly. We will also discuss credit scores and how to use them to your advantage by building a good score and avoiding ruining your financial reputation.

WHAT IS CREDIT AND HOW DOES IT WORK?

Credit is essentially a type of loan that allows you to buy things now and pay for them later. Credit means you are borrowing money that will need to be paid back. The most critical thing to know and remember is that, *depending on how long it takes you to pay off this debt, you might have to pay back more than you initially borrowed because of the interest rate associated with the loan.* The longer it takes you to pay off that loan, the more money you end up paying for that product due to the interest that accumulates.

Using credit can be very useful for large purchases, like homes or cars since it isn't easy to pay for those items all at once with cash. But, you will need to have built up a good credit score to buy these large items on credit.

Credit Score

So what the heck is a credit score, and why is it so important? Everyone has a credit score, and it's important to understand what yours is and how it works. *Your credit score is based on how well you've been able to pay back your loans and credit in the past.* If you pay your credit card off each month when it is due, you will begin to build up a good reputation and, therefore, a good credit score. The higher your score, the easier it will be to borrow larger amounts of money.

This score also affects your ability to get a loan, rent an apartment, and even get a job. Essentially, it is a number that represents your reputation for being responsible when it comes to borrowing and repaying money. You improve this score by making your payments on time, keeping your balances low, and sometimes paying slightly more than what is due.

Types of Credit

Credit comes in different forms, from credit cards to mortgages and personal loans. Credit cards are useful for smaller purchases, whether it be a few hundred or a few thousand dollars. Mortgages are almost always reserved for buying a house, building a house, or refurbishing your current home.

Personal loans are usually larger loans you take out to pay for whatever you need. The amounts for which you qualify for each of these credit-based loans will depend on many things. Your age, salary, credit score, and the length of repayments will all play a role in how much you can borrow.

How Credit Cards Work

Credit cards are connected to financial institutions like banks and credit unions. They are whom you are borrowing money from when you use the credit card. These cards allow you to borrow money up to a certain limit. This limit is determined by your credit score. You must always pay off your credit card balance for exactly what you have spent.

Remember, over time, interest will be added to these borrowed amounts, which means you are paying back more than you originally used. Depending on the specific terms of the credit card you are using, you might also have to pay an annual fee or bank charges as well. Make sure to research and be aware of the terms of every credit card you use, so you can pay it off with the least amount of additional interest cost.

Secured vs. Unsecured Credit Cards

When you decide to take out a credit card, you'll notice there are two types, secured and unsecured. These are the most common types and come with a unique set of rules.

Secured: With these cards, you're expected to pay a deposit at the beginning, which acts as a safety net for them if you miss a payment. It's important that you don't rely on your deposit during the months you're in a financial pinch. Your goal should always be to pay off your credit card debt first. When you decide to close your credit card, the institution will give you your deposit back if you never allow your payments to lapse.

Unsecured: Unsecured cards don't expect a deposit in the beginning, but they usually charge higher interest rates that will cost you more if you can't make your payments on time. They also tend to offer lower credit limits to ensure you don't rack up too much debt that you aren't able to pay.

In both cases, secured and unsecured, there tends to be a loyalty program offering you some form of discount or loyalty reward each time you make a purchase. For example, you might hear about a certain percent "cash back" on every purchase. This is an initiative to encourage you to spend money, but it is also a great way for you to get something back. Again, it is important to understand all of the details of the credit card you choose to help avoid additional charges and a bad score for your money's reputation.

HOW TO USE CREDIT RESPONSIBLY (AND WHY IT MATTERS)

"Using credit responsibly" means never spending more than you have. Even when you have a high credit limit, that doesn't mean you should reach that limit, otherwise known as "maxing out." This limit is the maximum amount the institution is comfortable lending you based on what they think you can reasonably afford. The first rule of thumb here is to *keep your balance below 30% of your limit so that you don't rack up high amounts of interest and fees.* So if you have a credit card and your limit is $500, try to cap yourself at $150.

This rule will help you afford your credit card and ensure you can pay off your account each month. This ties into the second rule of using credit responsibly, which is to always pay on time. Remember that good reputation and good credit we discussed? Well, if you don't pay your account on time, you will hurt your credit score, and you could also face penalties. These are costs and stressors you can avoid burdening yourself with if you always make it a priority to remember to apply these two rules. By keeping the credit limit low and setting reminders to make your payments on time, you'll be able to use the credit card to your benefit, and your credit score will strengthen.

The goal should be to build up that good credit which will then help you along the way with larger purchases. When applying for a credit card, start with one and use the two rules mentioned above to practice healthy usage. Also, practice the strategy of differentiating between *wants* and *needs* when using your credit card. Using these strategies will save you a lot of fees and charges down the line. Keep it simple and paid off. It's tempting to open more credit cards since they all have great loyalty programs and discounts, but remember that it is just a marketing tool to get you to spend more.

While we suggest you always pay the full amount due before making more purchases, it's important to at least pay the very minimum. The amount you are required to pay each month isn't the total you've spent on the card; it's a percentage of it. This is the very least you have to pay to ensure your credit score stays intact. But remember that the remaining amount will compound interest and fees, so it's best to pay off as much as you can.

Tips for New Credit Card Owners

Get Rid of Unnecessary Expenses

By reducing unnecessary expenses in your life, you'll be less inclined to use your credit card for purchases. So, rethink your expenses if you have any subscriptions you don't benefit from (like Netflix) or you're constantly buying takeout, coffee, or lunch. If you just spend on what you really need, you'll have more than enough left over each month, reducing your need for credit card purchases. Again, this is using the "wants" versus "needs" mindset when it comes to spending your money.

Make a Budget and Stick to It

Tying into point number one, by sticking to your budget, you'll have enough money for everything, and you avoid being forced to use your credit card or other forms of credit borrowing.

Your budget will show you where you're spending too much and how much you have allocated to each category in your life. I cannot emphasize enough how powerful creating and using a budget is for managing your money. If you can follow the plan and only spend the amount of money you've budgeted for each item, you should never need to depend on credit borrowing to get through the month. Use your budget to maintain your spending plan and control your money.

Shop Around for Lower Interest Rates

Not all credit cards are the same, and some may offer better rates than others. Before settling on one, look at all your options and see who offers the lowest rates. Your goal is to pay as few fees as necessary, so find an institution that offers the best cost. Pay back any money you borrowed with your credit card every month to avoid adding to that cost by paying high rates and fees.

Don't Use Your Credit Card Unless You've Paid in Full

This is a great tip to keep your spending within your means. Until you've paid off the remaining balance on your card, set a rule for yourself that you can't use the card until it's paid in full.

Avoid Cash Advances

"Cash advances" are essentially drawing money from the ATM with your credit card. This sounds like a good idea if you're in trouble, but these advances have some of the highest fees, and you can end up paying a lot of money for borrowing this way. With the amounts you withdraw, you can pay anything between 20% and 25% for that withdrawal. Meaning if you withdraw $1,000, you would have to pay back $1,250 at the very least. It's just not a good idea and should be avoided unless under very extreme circumstances, as it can cost you a lot of money quickly.

Set Up Automatic Payments

Just like with your savings accounts, you can set up automatic payment plans for your credit too. This means that every month money will be sent from your bank to your line of credit to pay what is due. This is the perfect way to ensure you stay up to date with payments without forgetting and falling behind. Remember that just being a few days late with payments can seriously damage your credit score, so this is well worth considering.

ACCESSING YOUR CREDIT SCORE

If you're curious to know your credit score and what you qualify for, some websites will allow you to access your score for free. You can download your credit report, which gives you a breakdown of your history, past loans, current loans, and other important financial information.

To access your report, simply research it online. For the US, check the governmental website, usa.gov, which provides all credit information. It's important to check your score at least once a year just to ensure all the information is correct. There are resources listed in the back of this book to help get you familiar with your score for free.

ACTIVITY

Take a moment to speak to your parents or guardians about credit cards and how they use them. We've covered a lot of information about how and why to use them, but it's always great to get some personal perspective on the matter. Make a list of the items your parents use their credit cards for, and separate those into what you think were *need* purchases and *want* purchases. Using your newfound knowledge, you'll see which of those were perhaps unnecessary. This is a great practice when it comes to navigating your own purchases. Who knows, you might have some good advice for your parents and how they are using their credit cards.

While you've learned all the ways to prevent certain unnecessary expenses, there are some that you just can't avoid—taxes are one of them. In the next chapter, we'll cover what taxes are, how they're calculated, and how to pay for them.

8

TAXES

This chapter will explore the basics of taxes, including why they exist and how to avoid common mistakes. It is a really smart idea to start learning about taxes when you are young. You are getting a jumpstart on understanding them and will be in a great position to navigate them as you get older. Unfortunately, schools usually don't teach us anything about taxes, so we head into adulthood without any real understanding or guidelines. So in this chapter, we'll look at how to pay taxes legally while possibly saving some money.

Why Tax Is Important

What exactly are taxes? The simplified definition of "tax" is that it is the money government collects from people and businesses to pay for things like roads, schools, and hospitals. It is collected money used to build and maintain the public places we access daily. These taxes are also used to help those in need, like after a natural disaster or families who live in lower-income households.

Why are taxes so important? Simply put, taxes are how we all chip in together to help maintain our communities, keep things in good shape and essentially take care of each other. Tax money is used to keep our society running smoothly. These taxes also allow the government to pay for our national defense, which is key to national safety.

While the idea of paying taxes each month is something most people hate doing, it's important to remember that without them, our quality of life would be significantly lower.

TYPES OF TAXES

There are three main types of taxes you will pay that apply to different parts of your life. You are taxed on the money you earn, taxed on what you purchase, and taxed on what you own.

What You Earn

The type of tax you're probably most familiar with and heard of most frequently is the one deducted from a person's salary each month. This is called Income Tax. This money is usually deducted from our salaries or wages by our employers, so we never really see the money. If you're self-employed, you will have to figure out your income tax yourself. The amount of tax you pay will depend on a few things, but mainly on how much you earn.

What You Buy

You also get taxed on the items you buy from the store. This is called <u>Sales Tax</u>. The prices you see on the shelves often already have the tax added so that you see what your total price would be. But if you look at the bottom of your receipt, it often shows how much of what you paid is tax. This is also known as valued added tax (VAT), where tax is added to most products at different stages of their production and packaging.

What You Own

If you own things like property or tangible items (like a house, machinery, or equipment), you will pay tax on those items. This is called <u>Property Tax</u>. Also, if you receive an inheritance from a family member, you will pay tax on that property or money. These taxes are hard to avoid since any transfer of these items or money into another person's name will, by default, initiate a tax payment.

THE EFFECT OF TAXES ON YOUR INCOME

Despite being a teenager, if you earn an income, you will still have to pay taxes. The tax rule isn't based on age but rather on income. As mentioned, the amount of tax you pay will depend on how much you earn. Higher percentages are taken from higher-income earners. Tax percentages are assigned to "tax brackets" or levels of income.

For instance, in 2022, the tax rate in the USA worked as follows:

- Incomes in the $0 to $10,275 tax bracket – paid 10% tax.
- Incomes in the $10,276 to $41,775 tax bracket – paid 12% tax.
- Incomes in the over $ 539,901-a-year tax bracket – paid 37% tax.

So while earning more money always sounds great, you have to remember that you will pay a higher percentage of tax on that money. The thinking here is that those who earn more can help out more.

TAX INCENTIVES & DEDUCTIONS

While taxes are unavoidable and a necessary part of our lives, there are a few strategies you can use to reduce your taxes. This is where tax deductions and incentives come into play. They are opportunities to reduce what we owe in taxes. There are some "incentives" that governments have put in place where you will pay less tax for taking certain actions. There are certain items you pay for that are considered "deductions," meaning that the government cannot tax you on them. Let's investigate this further.

Individual Tax Incentives

So, as I explained, you can be taxed on the amount of income you earn. But there are a few tax-deductible items. Tax-deductible items are *things you spend money on, which you can then deduct that cost from your total taxable income*. This is beneficial because by reducing your total taxable income, you are reducing the amount of tax you have to pay.

For example, paying for college is often tax deductible.

If in one year, your total taxable income was $20,000 and you paid $1,500 to go to college, your taxable income will be $20,000 - $1,500, bringing your total taxable income down to $18,500 and therefore reducing what you will owe for tax on your income.

Here is a list of considered tax-deductible items, which means you can deduct those amounts from your total taxable income. Some of the most common items that will apply to you include:

- Lifetime learning credit (tuition fees, coursework, and learning materials).
- Student loan interest deductions (you can deduct up to $2,500 if you pay student loans).
- Charitable donations deductions (you can subtract the value of items you bought or money you donated for charity).
- Medical expenses (there is a certain amount you can deduct annually).

- 401(k) (which is the retirement plan you don't pay taxes on).

To be able to deduct these items, it's important that you keep the receipts for everything as proof for when you submit your taxes. There are many apps available that can help you keep track of these receipts and purchases as well. If nothing else, just understanding the concept of tax deductions is a fantastic start as a teenager.

Businesses

Businesses tend to benefit from incentives more than individuals. Even so, it's important to be aware of them in general for the future. The amount a business pays in taxes can be reduced by incorporating certain strategies around how the business is run.

There are incentives for how businesses invest in new equipment, hire new employees, or make charitable donations. In many countries, especially in Europe, businesses are taxed on their amount of carbon emissions (which are harmful to the planet). So those businesses that decide to use greener energy will also save on taxes.

Before expecting to benefit from these incentives, knowing all the rules and how they work is important. This can take some extra time and research, but if you are interested in being a business owner, it is well worth your time to understand how tax incentives work.

HEALTHY TAX HABITS

If you want to make the most of your taxes, there are a few useful tips you can carry with you throughout your life.

Stay Organized throughout the Year

Although you only have to pay your taxes once a year, you don't want to get caught up at the last minute, scrambling to collect all your receipts. You won't possibly remember all your expenses throughout the year, making it difficult to gather all the information you need to get money back for your non-taxable items. Keep a folder, booklet, app, or spreadsheet to help you, and try to track your items on a daily or weekly basis.

Keep Track of Any Donations You Might Make

While you want to donate money to enhance the lives of others, there is no reason why you shouldn't reap the tax benefits of being charitable. Ensure you keep all the receipts and information regarding your donations.

Find Tax Breaks You Qualify For

Do your research and find out what your expenses are and how many of them are not taxable. You might be surprised to find out how many of those items you can save on.

Talk to a Professional

It is always a good idea to consult a professional about any matter, and tax is no different. Speak to someone in the industry and get some advice on what you think you may qualify for. You can also use these professionals to help you file taxes the first few times. Many businesses specialize in taxes, so they will help you file yours correctly. It's well worth trying the first few times to do it yourself.

File Your Taxes on Time

There are specific dates by which your taxes have to be filed. Always ensure it is done on time to avoid any penalties. By keeping track of it all year round, you are more likely to get it done in time.

Most of All, Don't Be Shady by Trying to Avoid Them

While there are strategies to legitimately reduce your taxable amount, they are not something that can be avoided—no matter how much you hate them. Don't think that it's something you should only worry about as an adult because putting it off can have significant consequences. Since tax money is used to keep our society running, the government does not take kindly to tax evasion. So be sure that you know what tax you have to pay, and make sure you pay it. Depending on where you live, tax evasion can lead to jail time, or they can even seize your passport. It's not worth it, so do the right thing and file your taxes.

COMMON QUESTIONS ABOUT TAX

If you're feeling nervous about starting your taxes, don't worry, that's normal. But it's important to start somewhere, and by finishing this chapter, you've taken the first step. Some common questions and answers will make the process a little easier to understand.

Do I Have to Pay Taxes for Jobs Like Babysitting or Lawn Mowing?

As you've probably realized, it's not really about your age or your job but more about the income you're earning. So if you earn more than $400 a year from these jobs, you will have to file taxes on this money. What's great is that there are a few deductibles you can claim back for that are directly related to your job. So any expenses, like getting to work, can be deducted.

What Is the Difference Between Gross Income and Net Income?

When you get a job, apply for a job, or start filing your taxes, you will work with terms like *gross income* or *net income*. These are just fancy terms used to describe your income before and after paying taxes and other deductions that automatically get taken off your salary. Your gross income is all the money you have before getting taxed. This is usually the amount they discuss in your job interview or that you see on your paycheck. Net income, however, is what you have left for yourself once these taxes and other amounts are deducted.

What Other Money Is Deducted from My Paycheck?

Depending on where you live, a few different deductions will be taken from your paycheck if you work a part-time or full-time job. These are usually automatic, so you don't have to worry about them. But in some cases, it is money deducted and set aside so that if you ever lose your job, you can claim it as your unemployment money.

What Do I Need to File Tax Returns?

There are a few documents you need to get in order if you want to start filing taxes. This is why it's a great idea to discuss your taxes with a professional and get some help the first time around. But the documents you're looking for are your tax ID and W-2 form (which gives a full breakdown of your salary or wages.)

ACTIVITY

If you're already earning a relatively stable income from a part-time job, it's a good idea to start preparing for taxes. You can keep all the receipts for your purchases and store your bank statements digitally. If you prefer storing your receipts digitally, too, try apps where you can store the information specifically for tax purposes. By slowly starting to collect the information, you will be better prepared for tax season.

Ask your parents or guardians for help in getting started. It's all about staying organized and prepared and, of course, getting some help from those who have done it before. Before you know it, you'll be an expert and file taxes in your sleep.

Congrats! You have done a lot of great work starting to understand critical basic money strategies like savings, budgets, compound interest, and even the basics of taxes. Now we will move on to a more modern money topic: digital currencies. The next chapter will cover the basics of cryptocurrencies, what they are, how they work, and how you can use them.

9

MODERN MONEY – CRYPTOCURRENCY BASICS

Every informed person needs to know about Bitcoin because it might be one of the world's most important developments.

— LEON LUOW

Cryptocurrency has become incredibly powerful and sought after in the past few years, and with good reason. It's one of the most exciting things to happen in our modern world, and most adults don't even truly understand it. Understand a world where you have complete control of your money. No banks or credit card companies tell you how to use your money. Welcome to the world of cryptocurrency.

WHAT IS CRYPTOCURRENCY?

Cryptocurrency is a digital currency that is protected with hyper-secure technology. The currency is also decentralized, which means it isn't under the control of governments or financial institutes.

Bitcoin is by far the most famous cryptocurrency and was also the first of its kind. It was first created in 2009, and to date, thousands of currencies have been established. Even if the world of cryptocurrency might not be something you are interested in at this time and seems kind of complicated, it is a really good idea to keep reading this chapter to gain even a basic understanding of concepts and terminologies.

HOW DO CRYPTOCURRENCIES WORK?

Cryptocurrencies are rather complicated, which is exactly what makes them so powerful. Essentially, these cryptocurrencies are based on blockchain technology. This means all users can access all the information at the same time, and no one owns the data or controls the data. Essentially, all the information is somewhere on the net, never at one specific place, owned by one specific person. These blockchains hold all kinds of information, from money to music and identities.

Why It's So Popular

Cryptocurrency has grown in popularity for many reasons. First and foremost is because you have specific control over your finances. We have so many authoritative figures in society telling us what we can and can't do, but cryptocurrencies are different. And that's one of the main reasons it's gaining so much traction.

The second reason is that it's not like fiat currencies. A fiat currency is a type of money that has no specific value and whose value changes with supply and demand. Most modern currencies we know, like the U.S. dollar, are fiat currencies. The difference between cryptocurrencies and fiat currencies is that fiat is influenced by anything government-related, like inflation. But cryptocurrencies are owned by nobody and are not affected by any political or governmental influences. This means that currencies like Bitcoin are much more stable in terms of value than currencies like the euro or dollar.

The third reason these currencies are becoming so popular is because of how private they are. With any other transaction that uses traditional currencies, each purchase is tracked and recorded. But for people who want no record of their purchases, Bitcoin is perfect. This can be helpful for people who live in countries with immense authoritarianism.

More and more businesses are accepting crypto like Bitcoin as a form of payment, and it is becoming a mainstream payment method. The value and popularity of these currencies are expected to continue climbing and may be accessible for almost all purchases.

HOW TO BUY CRYPTOCURRENCY

Find a Source

First, find a source. If you're interested in buying cryptocurrency, whether it be for investments or purchases, there are different ways of doing it. To do it safely and accurately, it is essential to buy your currency from safe and reliable sources.

Brokers: Working through a broker is a failproof way of ensuring you're buying legit cryptocurrency. These brokers allow you to buy and sell cryptocurrencies, as well as other investments like stocks or commodities. While they tend to have the lowest costs for buying cryptocurrency, they are also limited in features. But as a new currency owner, this is a safe place to begin.

Cryptocurrency Exchanges: These platforms offer different features of the cryptocurrency market, including things like "wallets" and interest-bearing accounts. If crypto is something that seriously interests you, it's best to explore these features by yourself and fully understand what all the terms mean.

Load Money onto Your Account

Second, once you've decided where you want to purchase your currency, you can go ahead and start funding your account. Usually, this means using your fiat currency to buy the cryptocurrency, which can often be done easily with a debit card. Buying crypto with credit cards is often considered very risky, and many financial institutions don't allow you to buy crypto with your card. But it's for the best anyway since you don't want to start your investment journey in debt.

Place Your Order

The third step includes placing an order for your currency. This is done through your broker or an app. When using the app, you simply have to select how much you want to buy and go ahead with your purchase. When you want to sell your assets, you can also simply select a sell button on the app or inform your broker.

You can use things like Bitcoin just as you would any other type of investment. If you buy a few coins today, you can simply keep them and sell them in a few years for a profit when the price increases. This is very common and can be done with any cryptocurrency available.

To give you an idea of the value, in 2010, you could buy Bitcoin for as little as $0.09. The value of this currency excelled, and in May 2022, it was valued at $28,305 apiece. That means that if you bought 20 Bitcoin in 2010, you paid just under $2 in total. Twelve years later, this $2 investment would be worth over $560,000. Remember how we discussed how even the smallest amount of savings each month could make a huge difference? In this context, I hope it makes sense that even the smallest amount can make the biggest difference. Not all $2 investments will turn into $500,000 returns, but you get the idea.

Five Popular Cryptocurrencies

If you're thinking about getting started with investing in cryptocurrencies, there are a few that have become rather popular and profitable in recent years. While this popularity means that their value has increased, it also means that they are a slightly safer investment. You can always try your luck with more unconventional currencies, but there is no telling whether these will bring you any return in the future.

So, with the help and guidance of someone who knows about crypto, choose a currency you're considering investing in and find out whether it seems like a solid idea. Also, be sure to run everything past your parents or guardians first.

Bitcoin: As mentioned, it is the first cryptocurrency and by far the most popular. Currently, the value of a Bitcoin stands at $16,846.

Ethereum: Ethereum is gaining popularity fast since it allows you to use the currency for a few different functions. The value is currently at $1,242.

Tether: Tether is a unique form of crypto, which is drawing more attention to it. It is known as a "stablecoin" since it is based on the value of a specific asset. In the case of Tether, the asset is the U.S. dollar. This is completely different from how Bitcoin operates. But what makes Tether unique is that it allows investors to move their money from one type of cryptocurrency to another. In the past, you would need to convert your Bitcoin to the dollar and then to your newly chosen cryptocurrency. But Tether allows you to do a transition without needing to convert the coins to dollars. Currently, the value of Tether is $1, and it will remain that way indefinitely.

BNB: BNB was originally created to pay for discounted trades. It has transformed into a traditional currency you can use to buy items or make online purchases. The price of BNB is currently $286.

USD Coin: The USD coin is similar to Tether in the idea that it is a stablecoin linked to the U.S. dollar with a fixed value of $1. The currency is backed by physical assets, so it is a stable way to buy and sell items online.

MISTAKES TO AVOID

Whether you're buying crypto for investing purposes or to use it as a currency, there are some mistakes you want to avoid. With anything new, you have to do your research and ensure you know the ins and outs to avoid making painful financial mistakes. Here are some common ones you can avoid:

Not Doing Your Research

If you're going to be investing your money in crypto, you have to ensure you do your research properly and at least learn the basics. Get to know exactly how it works, what will be expected from you, and what you can expect from it. There are a lot of learning opportunities out there, so at least do the very minimum. Not knowing the basics of the investment you're getting involved in can be detrimental.

Not Researching Fees

Part of doing your research means getting to know what fees are involved. When buying crypto, there are some fees in different parts of the process that you have to get to know. If you don't, you can pay a lot more than you have to. For instance, if you buy crypto with a credit card, you might end up paying more than if you bought it in cash. Find out what the most affordable ways are of investing and check for any additional fees you are unaware of.

Investing for Immediate Returns

When you decide to invest in crypto, you have to know it's going to be a long-term game. If you want to truly make a return on your money, you have to be willing to leave the money for years. So don't invest in crypto if you're looking for a quick buck. See it as your investment in your future, with little to no immediate results. This is especially true if you see that the value of your investment is dropping—your instinct would be to withdraw your money to avoid further loss. But if you do your research well and understand that it is a long-term game, chances are the investment will gain value again. And the longer it stays, the more it grows in value. So don't invest in crypto with the idea of making money within the next few months.

Storing Your Crypto Online

Part of the basic research you will do is finding out about how crypto is stored. They are often stored in something called a "digital wallet," which can be online or offline on hardware. You are much better off storing your digital wallet offline on a hard drive or USB stick. Storing your wallet online opens the door for hackers and can be much riskier. Find out how you can protect yourself, which may include offline storage.

Not Saving Your Crypto Password

To store your crypto, you will be required to enter a password or seed phrase. But unlike most logins that allow you to recover your password, crypto wallets don't let you easily recover your password. So it is crucial to saving it somewhere private and somewhere safe, or you might lose your investment. There is a Bitcoin investor who cannot access a $321 million Bitcoin investment because he forgot his password. You don't want to be that person, so be smart about your password.

Opening Opportunities for Scammers

It is too easy to be scammed if you have a crypto investment, so avoid it at all costs. The hackers use different phishing techniques to try to access your investments. Again, that's why it's best to store your money offline. But also, avoid scammers who might ask for your personal information via apps, emails, or calls.

In the next chapter, we'll look at the most common mistakes beginners make when it comes to personal finance. We'll learn about the dangers of debt, how to avoid common money traps, and what to do if you find yourself in financial trouble. This chapter is an important one as it can prevent a lot of lost time and money if you learn these lessons the hard way. So learn the easy way and just keep reading!

10

SIX BIGGEST ROOKIE MONEY MISTAKES TO AVOID

Avoid being dead broke!

With something as complex as finances, you are bound to make some mistakes, run into obstacles, and be uncertain about what to do. It's part of the process and is so important in making progress. It's important to make mistakes and face some obstacles so you can learn and improve from there on. That being said, some mistakes aren't necessary and can be avoided with some guidance. By learning from other people's mistakes, you don't have to go through the pain of learning it yourself.

Here are some common mistakes that you can and should avoid:

Impulse Buying

One of the best things you can do for your finances in your teens and throughout your adult life is to think about the purchase you want to make and whether it's something you want or need. Impulse buying is so easy in today's society, whether it be in a store or online. But before you add the item to your cart (digital or physical), think about whether this is an impulse buy or a necessity.

You can create a rule that if you need an item or really want it, you can only buy it if you're willing to go back to the store to buy it. Or, with online purchases, if you're still thinking about it in five to seven days, then you can buy it. But most of the time, we see something we like and immediately just purchase it. This causes a lot of financial stress, unnecessary spending, and less money for future goals. So by sticking to those rules regarding impulse purchases, you can save yourself a ton of money.

Putting Off Saving until Tomorrow

There is always a better time to do something. There is always a time when you'll have more money, more time, and more opportunities, so why start now?

That kind of mindset can set a person back—I know; I've been there. But as you've seen continuously throughout the book, there is no better time to start than right now. Too many adults (and teens) put off their financial planning until they're older, more settled, or have a bigger paycheck.

As a teenager, it's easy to say you're not earning enough yet, so you'll start when you're older. As young adults, it's easy to say you first want to find your feet, and then you'll start saving or investing. As parents, it's easy to say we can't invest because we have our kids to take care of. And as you continuously find a way to justify postponing it, it will never happen.

Making Major Purchases without Comparing Prices

I briefly discussed how important it is to compare the prices of credit companies or savings accounts. But it should be a rule you set for yourself to compare the prices of everything before buying it. This is especially useful for larger purchases, like a car. The market is full of companies fighting for customers, so there will always be a business selling the product at a better price or with more benefits. Don't make the mistake of buying the first option you see. Whether it is a car you're looking at, insurance types, or even clothing, be sure to check your options first.

You could save yourself so much money each month by just taking the time to compare your options once.

Maintaining Memberships

Are you paying for your own YouTube subscription, Spotify, Hulu, or Netflix accounts? Are you using them regularly enough to justify paying for them? If it's not adding any value to your life, don't waste your money on it. Instead, take those dollars and add them to your savings account and secure yourself for a better, wealthier future! And not only will you save money by not paying for subscriptions, but you will have more time to continue your growth and knowledge. Spend your time learning about investing, finances, or other skills. Don't see your canceled memberships as a loss. Instead, see it as money you save and the time you've gained to become the person you've always wanted to be.

Bumping Up Your Lifestyle with Each Paycheck

We tend to do this thing where we buy more because we earn more. This is very common with your first paycheck, and if you don't become aware of this, you'll do it with each promotion and raise you get. Essentially, we think because we earn more, we should stay in bigger homes or drive better cars. We start shopping at more expensive stores or going out to dinners more often. It's very common in society and one of the reasons that people get stuck financially.

But this is where your budget can save you and prevent you from getting into this rut. Stick to your budget and your amounts, no matter what you earn. Don't increase your spending because you get a pay increase. Instead, use that extra money for savings or investments. The less you spend and the more you save, the better off you'll be in the long run.

Not Checking for Hidden Fees

If you're taking out a loan, opening a credit card, or buying a car, be sure to check for hidden fees. The fine print can sometimes be extremely deceptive, and you'll be charged for things you didn't realize were included. Here are some of the most common places to find hidden fees, so you'll know what to look out for:

Account Maintenance Fees: These are very common bank fees, and despite not giving you a clear idea of what it really is, you can't really avoid these fees. They are automatically deducted from your account, so just understand that they exist with almost all banks.

Online Banking Fees: These fees are several transactions you perform with your online or banking app. The fees will differ from bank to bank but are most commonly for things like electronic transfers.

Card Replacement Fees: If you ever lose or break your card, don't think you'll get a replacement at no cost. These fees usually include the physical cost of the card and the cost of sending it to you.

Overdraft Fees: This isn't something you may have to worry about just yet, but it is something to remember if you ever do open an overdraft account. Essentially, an overdraft is a type of credit that allows you to spend more money than what you physically have in your account. But as with most credits, you will be charged for 'loaning' this money.

Early Closure Fees: If you open an account just for the rewards and then close it soon after, the bank will charge you a fee.

Inactivity Fees: If you have a bank account you haven't used in a while, you will be charged a fee. Keeping these accounts open requires admin on the end of the bank, which they will need to compensate for with your account fees. So if you have a bank account you no longer use, closing it instead of just leaving it dormant is best.

There are several things to watch out for when buying things like cars or other major items. These can range from advertising fees, documentation fees, sales tax, gap insurance, and more. So the rule is always to check for hidden fees in every single situation.

Paying Off the Wrong Debt First

This sounds counterintuitive, right? How can paying off your debt be a mistake? Well, the secret is knowing how to pay off the right debt first. If you have a few different sources of debt, whether it be in your teenage years or in the years to come, prioritize your debts. If you have extra money that you want to use to pay off your debts, it's best to aim for the ones that have the highest interest rates. If you have more than one credit card, pay off the one that charges you the most. When you get older, you can use this same mindset and pay off debts like student loans first since they tend to carry the most interest.

Buying Something Because It Sounds Like a Good Deal

There is nothing wrong with buying something at a discount because it is a way of saving money, right? But that is only true if it is something you were already planning on buying or that you need. Simply buying something because it is on sale doesn't save you anything. You spent money on an item that wasn't in your budget, which does not mean you saved money. If you can view all your purchases like that, you will save yourself tons of money by *not* buying things simply because they're on sale.

Not Investing in the Future

If you haven't already understood the importance of investing in the future just yet, I'm going to use this opportunity to emphasize it one more time. It's *really* important. For the power of compound interest to truly work in your favor, start saving as soon as possible. The rookie mistake too many people make is waiting for the future before they start saving. It's an easy mistake to make, but it often creates a postponement for years and years, taking away the opportunity to build compound interest.

Not Paying Off Debt

One of the worst rookie mistakes adults make too often, which you can avoid now already, is not paying off your debt as soon as possible. Whether you have a student loan or a credit card, you should try paying them off as soon as possible. Don't just make the minimum payments each month—try to prioritize paying them off quickly. The longer you have these debts, the more interest and fees you build up, and you spend months or years paying a lot more than you originally owed.

Many experts suggest that paying off your debt completely should be your number one priority, even above saving money. It makes sense if you consider how much money you're losing due to high interest rates. But instead, pay off as much as you can while also putting money into a savings account. If you want to pay your debt off quicker, rather try cutting other expenses and using that money for the debt.

Maxing Out Credit Cards

In the chapter about credit cards, we discuss how important it is to keep your credit below 30% of your limit. If you spend your entire limit, you are setting yourself up for tremendous struggles. Maxing out your credit card means you not only have to pay back that entire amount, but you also have to pay back the interest on that amount. And what often happens is that the monthly payment is so high that most people can only afford to pay back the absolute minimum. And by only paying the minimum, you aren't able to pay off the credit, and you're stuck in this loop of endless credit and fees. You need to be able to pay off more than the minimum to quickly pay off the credit. But with maximum credit and maximum fees, you're making it nearly impossible for yourself. Nothing ruins the potential for financial stability more than this seemingly small mistake.

Not Saving for Emergencies

Not having money saved for emergencies is a rookie mistake, and you know why it's important. Having money stored away for unexpected events will be a lifesaver. So don't make this rookie mistake and postpone this sort of savings plan for the future. Emergencies can happen to anyone at any age, and you want to be ready. And if you're not ready, you may end up paying for emergencies with credit cards, which will be one of the worst mistakes you can make financially. Avoid this at all costs, and just simply prioritize your emergency savings.

Not Tracking Net Worth

To calculate your net worth, you have to calculate what you have (assets) and subtract items that cost you money (liabilities). Assets can be anything like property or investments, while liabilities are your debts. It's important to know what your net worth is so that you can see how your financial situation progresses over time. The growth of your net worth will be a great indicator of how you're succeeding with your financial goals.

Remember, you can't measure what you don't track, so track your net worth and use it as motivation and a feeling of accomplishment.

Allowing Money Munchers into Your Life

A money muncher is essentially a term for something you really don't have money for and haven't budgeted for, but you've allowed it to take priority over your goals. Money munchers come in different forms for different people, but we easily justify them. We tend to buy them and think, *"It's okay if I buy this. I'll just spend less on clothes this month."* Or you might tell yourself you'll work an extra shift to compensate for the money you spent on this.

The rule should be simple: if it's not in the budget, you shouldn't buy it. If you really want it, it's best to save up for it a month or two in advance. But don't buy it first and tell yourself you'll find a way to compensate. That never works, believe me. And you're sacrificing some amazing opportunities in the future.

ACTIVITY

Looking at these common mistakes, are there any you recognize and feel you've made before? Make a list of the ones you've made a few times, and create a column for potential solutions. For instance, impulse buying is something many of us face on a daily basis. So write down ways you can prevent impulse buying, like taking coffee when you leave the house to prevent buying it at Starbucks. Or, if you're not tracking your net worth, use the opportunity to start. Going forward, list some of these mistakes you want to avoid in the future, and use this to motivate you to manage your money correctly in the future.

In the last chapter, we are going to go over some basics about retirement. As a teenager, it may seem a little early to be discussing this topic. However, I would encourage you to start thinking about retirement as: "planning to be financially independent as soon as possible so I don't have to work anymore." Thinking, planning, and strategizing about retirement when you are a teenager can help you get there sooner than later—so read on!

11

RETIREMENT

The question isn't at what age I want to retire, it's at what income.

— GEORGE FOREMAN

This chapter is all about retirement planning, how it works, how much you need, and what sort of investments you need to get started. If you've found yourself wondering, "why should teens even worry about retirement," consider the example of compound interest. If you're starting as a teen, you'll be saving more, working less as an adult, and enjoying the fruit of your labor at a younger age.

You may think it's way too early to start thinking about retirement, but it's one of the most important financial decisions you can make. Set yourself ahead and embrace this chapter.

WHY START THINKING ABOUT RETIREMENT

There are a few reasons that saving for retirement early is a great idea. Other than the fact that you'll be able to retire earlier, you'll have more to retire with. Remember, retirements work as a type of savings plan where you add money, allowing it to grow and gain interest. When you're ready to retire, that will be the money you'll use to live off. So if you're starting at a young age, you have more years to add more money and could retire earlier if that money is enough.

The concept of compound interest comes in perfectly here since you saw how powerful it is when you start early. So the earlier you start, the more you will compound over time. Even the smallest amount of investments each month is better than nothing. You don't have to earn a lot and add thousands to the account each month—even just a few dollars is worth it.

While retirement seems like forever away, it's never too early to start. Before you know it, you'll be a grown adult with adult responsibilities and expenses, making it harder to put away extra money each month. So use your youth and fewer responsibilities as a way to build up a good retirement fund. By starting now, you'll set yourself up for a comfortable future.

DIFFERENT WAYS TO SAVE FOR RETIREMENT

There isn't a single best method to choose from. Understanding these different options will allow you the freedom to choose something that works best for you.

Ask Your Parents to Set Up a Savings Account For You

This savings account can be retirement-specific, which prevents you from accessing the money. It is built for long-term savings, which often also comes with slightly higher interest rates. Again, the key is not depositing large amounts; it's about getting started and doing what you can.

Get a Part-Time Job and Automatically Deposit Money into Your Savings Account

If you have this savings account open, you can set up an automated savings plan that sends money from your bank account each month without you having to do it. This means you never see that money, making it less likely that you'll feel like spending it. You don't have to save all of it, of course. Just a portion should be sent to the savings account so that you have some money to enjoy in your day-to-day.

Start a Side Hustle to Earn Extra Money for Retirement

In Chapter 2, you've learned all about extra income avenues and how you can use this money to save for your financial goals. If you have your priorities set on saving for retirement, this is a great reason to start that side hustle we've discussed. Since the retirement fund doesn't have a short-term timeframe, you have the opportunity to get your side hustle started and get it running without feeling pressured to earn money from it for your retirement. You can put each little bit you make from the side hustle into your retirement fund without having strict amount goals.

Invest in Stocks, Bonds, or Other Financial Instruments

Investments are a great place to start setting up your pension money. Since some of these investments can grow tremendously (like with Apple), you have the opportunity to rapidly build up a retirement fund. It's just important to remember that money you withdraw from most investments is taxable, whereas specific retirement plans aren't. So whatever you have in investments, remember that a portion of that money won't be yours since it will be taxed.

Live below Your Means

We've discussed this earlier in the book, and it perfectly fits in with your retirement too. To have money to save for your retirement, it's not necessarily about earning more money. It's about better managing what you already have. So living below your means and spending less (specifically on unnecessary items) so that you can use that money wisely for the future.

Make a Budget So You Know Where Your Money Is Going

A budget is important—have you noticed? To successfully start saving for retirement, setting a budget is the first step. You will have better control of your expenses and, as a result, better control over your savings opportunities. If you can start and manage a budget in your teens, imagine the control you'll have in your adult life.

COMMON RETIREMENT QUESTIONS YOU SHOULD KNOW

What Happens If I Don't Save Enough Before I Retire?

The point of saving early for retirement is to have enough money for when you decide to stop working. But what happens the day you're ready to retire and don't have enough money to stop working?

There are a few things that can happen or that should be done when this occurs. Firstly, you might have to keep working longer than you planned, meaning you'll be well into your sixties and still working. The other option is to downsize your lifestyle to reduce your expenses so that you have enough to sustain yourself.

In situations where those options aren't viable, asking friends and family for support, taking out a loan, or selling your possessions are also possible. The thing about these options is that they aren't ones you want to rely on. Nobody wants to downsize their lifestyle, work longer than necessary, or depend on family for money. So use that as motivation to get started now and start building your pension fund.

At What Age Do You Retire?

Generally, across most countries, the retirement age is 65. But this age can change depending on the person's individual situation. Some may retire earlier since they were able to create a large enough fund to retire. Others may need to work longer if they don't have a savings plan in place.

ACTIVITY

Take five minutes to envision the sort of life you want when you retire. Write down what your day-to-day would look like, the places you'll travel to, and the things you'd like to own. Make the picture as clear and detailed as possible. Then, think about the type of money that lifestyle would require. You can take it a step further and start calculating and estimating how much you'd need to invest each year to get to that amount. Use this image of your lifestyle as a driving force to get yourself to save your money.

In the next chapter, you'll learn about savings plans for rainy days and what that entails.

12

RAINY DAYS

Preparing for life's curveballs.

If you've ever heard about insurance before, you probably know it's rather valuable and can be a lifesaver in unforeseen circumstances - a.k.a. curveballs. Everyone should have insurance, and it's never too early to start learning about how, why, and when.

WHAT IS INSURANCE

Insurance is a way of covering costs in the case of an unfortunate event, like an accident, robbery, or natural disaster. It's a way of covering yourself in the case of a very costly emergency without needing thousands of dollars in the bank.

Essentially, insurance are run by companies that manage everyone's monthly payments. When an accident happens, the company pays out money from that pool of everyone's savings. This pool of money is replenished every time "customers" (known as policyholders) add money by paying their insurance fees.

We need to have insurance to protect us in the event of a disaster, accident, or injury.

There are different types of insurance for different situations, and you have the opportunity to choose the type of insurance that best fits your situation. If you don't own a car, it won't make sense to have car insurance. So selecting which insurance you should take out depends on you. But here are the different types and what they cover:

Health Insurance

As the name implies, health insurance covers all kinds of medical costs, from doctor's visits to hospital stays and medications. Different types of health insurance options cover different costs. Some of the cheaper options won't cover as many expenses. But the more expensive insurance options will cover things like dental visits or even plastic surgery. So the type of health insurance you take out will depend on the coverage you want and your budget.

Life Insurance

Life insurance is a type of insurance that covers your death and pays out money to your chosen beneficiaries. So when you take out life insurance, you decide what percentage of your insurance gets paid to different people in your life. In some cases, your life insurance can also cover any debt you have, like your mortgage. But you shouldn't wait too long to take out life insurance since you tend to pay less for your premiums when you're young. Starting in your twenties, you can begin to look at options which means you will pay less and still have that coverage if something happens. Once again, the power of compound interest comes into play, highlighting how important it is to start any savings plan early.

Disability Insurance

Disability insurance is something that pays out in the case of an emergency where you aren't able to work due to a disability. This is crucial to have because if something ever had to happen to you and you weren't able to work, being covered financially is crucial.

This isn't something that enough people think about, but it is really important. Accidents can happen in a second and can steal a lot from your life. You don't want to add to that stress or burden by not being able to bring in some source of income. So make this a priority when you're older.

Homeowners Insurance (or Rental Insurance)

As a homeowner, you have the physical building and all the furniture inside. If something like a fire, natural disaster, or robbery had to happen, you would want insurance that pays the value of those items. So the homeowner's insurance covers your house and the furniture in the case of such an emergency. For renters, the same happens, but it will only be the items in the house that you rent, not the building itself.

Auto Insurance

If you own a car, auto insurances protect your car in the case of an accident or robbery. In the case of an accident with another car, there are often situations where you would also need to pay for the other person's damages, which can become extremely costly. So auto insurance ensures you get paid out if something happens to the car. It's important to know that these insurances don't cover the costs of maintaining the car.

Travel Insurance

In situations where you have to travel abroad, travel insurance is great to have since it covers you in case something happens while you're away. These differ from company to company, but usually cover your medical expenses and sometimes even your luggage. These are short-term insurances that are usually paid just before you leave or sometimes during your stay abroad.

DIFFERENT INSURANCE TERMS TO UNDERSTAND

When you look at different insurances, they use pretty much the same lingo, which can sometimes be confusing. Here are some common words used in the insurance world that are worth understanding already:

Premium: This is the cost you will pay each month for your policy. This amount can differ based on many different things, from your age, gender, health, income, and risk. When it comes to car premiums, the price is determined based on the type of car you have and even the color and make. So there is no fixed price, but it is all based on your individual situation.

Policy Limit: It's important to know what your policy limit is since it is the maximum amount your insurer will pay out to you. If it's car insurance, there will be a limit they pay out, no matter what the costs are of the accident. If it is health insurance, it is the maximum amount the insurer pays out, no matter what your hospital fees are. It's important to know these amounts so you can be prepared for any expenses you'll have to cover. You can take out a policy that has higher limits or pays for all your costs, but they naturally come with higher monthly premiums.

Deductibles: Even though your insurer will pay out in the case of an accident, you will still need to pay a minimum amount (known as a deductible) before they pay out your claim. This prevents customers from going to the insurer for even the smallest claim. So, for instance, if you scratch your car, your deductible may be $300. If the scratch only costs $100 to fix, you would rather pay for the repairs yourself than pay a $300 deductible so your insurer can cover the repair costs.

WHAT INSURANCE TO CONSIDER AS A TEEN

With all these options available, how do you know which ones you should start considering and which to leave for the future?

At the very least, you need medical or health insurance to cover your costs in the case of medical expenses. Ask your parents whether you have medical insurance, and if you don't, speak to them about getting insured. While possessions can always be replaced, your health should not be compromised.

Of course, if you have a car or are considering getting one soon, auto insurance is a great idea. As a young driver, you want to be covered so that you aren't out of pocket (or out of a vehicle) if something happens. Different companies will offer different rates and fees. So don't be afraid to ask around and get different quotes from different companies to find the best price and option that suits your situation and budget.

As for the rest, you can add these types of insurance as you add more possessions and responsibilities to your life. When you become a renter, you can take out rental insurance. And when you start building a family, you can consider taking out life insurance. These insurances don't all have to come at once, and you don't have to feel overwhelmed by them all.

Add them to your life one at a time as they become relevant. They can be lifesavers in different situations, so be sure to add them as soon as they become relevant.

COMMON INSURANCE MISTAKES TO AVOID

Although your highest priority isn't necessarily taking out insurance, it is worth knowing what the common mistakes are to avoid them in the future. And who knows, perhaps you can speak to your parents about these and find out if they're making any mistakes you can advise them on.

Not Knowing How Much Insurance to Take Out

Whether it is for your car, your health, or your home, it's important to shop around for the best price, and perhaps get a second opinion about what a good coverage amount is.

Not Having Enough Coverage

One of the things that can happen if you don't know how much coverage to take is that you might take out too little. And as a result, you won't be covered for certain accidents or situations. When it comes to insurance, you really want to get to know all the details about everything. You want to fully understand what you need and what your premium covers. Nothing is worse than thinking you're covered and then you're not.

Having Too Much Coverage

Again, the importance of asking the right questions and the right people cannot be overstated. Sometimes companies will cover you for way more than you could need, which pushes your premiums sky-high. But it's important to ask them for a complete breakdown of everything you're covered for. You don't want to be covered for things that would never apply to you. Some examples would be an auto insurance policy that charges you more because your vehicle is parked on the street, but in fact, your car is parked in the garage every night. Or having medical insurance that covers you for illnesses that don't fit your profile.

ACTIVITY

Speak to your parents about their insurance and what you're covered for. And ask them which ones they've had to use in the past. This tends to open up great conversations and stories and will show you just how handy these can be for getting out of trouble.

Knowing what insurances are available in the future will help you prepare for it. But insurances aren't the only thing to prepare for—there are some purchases you should also be ready for, which we will cover in the next chapter.

13

EIGHT MAJOR PURCHASES TO PLAN FOR

As a teenager, there are so many great things to look forward to in your future. There are items, activities, and experiences you can look forward to and already start planning for—from your first laptop to your first car, apartment, college tuition, and so much more.

The thing about these purchases is that you rarely realize how much money you actually need to purchase these items. And by the time you realize it, it's usually too late. This chapter is going to teach you all about the items you need to start planning for and how to get started.

YOUR FIRST CAR

If you don't already have one, you probably can't wait to get your first car. There is no better symbol of independence for a young adult than a car, so there is good reason to be excited.

But you have to know what you're in for! Beyond the excitement, it is important to know what you need to prepare for. Other than actually financing and buying the car, there are a lot of other expenses that come with it. The most obvious cost is the gasoline to get from point A to point B. But there are also the costs of insurance, repairs, and maintenance.

So if you're saving up for a car, you will need to save enough to buy the car. But your monthly budgeting must also allow for the other expenses.

YOUR FIRST DEPOSIT

Before buying your own home, chances are you will be renting an apartment or a home for a few years. These carry many costs, and it's important to be prepared for them. Of course, the first furniture is going to need some financing. But other than your physical items, you will also need to save for the deposit. Most rentals require a deposit from you in case you cause damage to the building. So apart from the first month's rent, you often have to pay a deposit before moving in. This can depend from landlord to landlord, but it is often the equivalent of one or two months' rent. So before getting ready to move into a place, you have to save up for those expenses.

YOUR FIRST HOME

One of the biggest purchases you will ever make in your life is a house. Whether you're buying a starter home or looking for a forever option, there are a lot of costs to consider that come with owning a home. The obvious cost is the money to buy the physical structure. But there are a few costs most newbies don't know about, and it is worth knowing about them so you can start planning for them.

There are costs involved in making the sale, which includes transferring the title from the previous owner to you. These could become rather hefty, especially if you had help from lawyers and brokers to transfer the title. Throughout your time as the owner, your costs will be recurring and may include things like property tax, homeowner's insurance, maintenance, and repairs.

So if you're dreaming about having your own house one day and you're creating a budget and savings plan, it's good to take all the expenses into account.

VACATIONS

You don't have to wait until retirement before traveling and going on vacation! You're probably going to want to travel and see places while you're young and able, so it's best to start planning for these with some savings. These trips can often become expensive if you take into account the cost of traveling (flying or driving), accommodation, and food—and of course, spending money. So the sooner you start saving for these vacations, the sooner you can start enjoying them and exploring different parts of the world.

A PET

If you already have your own pet or plan on getting one in the future, it's something to plan for financially. Pets will cost money, so it's something worth noting when thinking of your future budgeting. Also, most pets have to be vaccinated and checked regularly by the vet. Their food, toys, medication, and vet bills will be a regular cost, so it's important to plan ahead.

A COLLEGE, GAP YEAR, OR VOCATIONAL SCHOOL

Whatever you decide to do after school, the earlier you start planning for it, the better. So if you're planning on going to college, you probably know it will be rather expensive and worth saving up for. There will be costs of tuition, books, and room and board. If you're looking to take a gap year, you will still need money to live off during that year, so it's best to start saving up. The money you save while you're still a teenager will take tremendous stress off yourself when you're older.

There are many ways to fund your tuition, including student loans with extremely high interest rates. If you take out student loans, chances are you will be paying them back for years and years. These loans will set you so far back in your financial journey. So whenever you can, with whatever you have, save up as much as you can for the tuition yourself. You don't want to have to rely on these student loans.

PERSONAL ITEMS: CLOTHES, LAPTOP, AND CELLPHONE

If you're planning on getting your first laptop or perhaps upgrading the ones you already have, it's worth saving up for it. These are major purchases and can often come with a hefty price tag. So save up a chunk of money to get these items for yourself.

The thing about these items is that you can buy them on credit a lot of the time. There are now ways to pay off your phone and laptop or open a clothing account for yourself. While it makes it easy to buy these items immediately, it also means you pay extensive fees for opening an account. So try as much as possible to rather save up for these items instead of using credit. Remember, the key with credit is to only use it for what you really need and keep your expenses below 30% of your limit.

YOUR FIRST INVESTMENT

If you enjoyed the chapter on investments and think it's something you'd like to do, you can already start saving for it. You have so many options to invest in stocks, bonds, and real estate to secure your financial future. So if it's something in your sights, prioritize your money and start planning for these.

THE UNEXPECTED CURVE BALLS

In this book, you learned that sometimes sh*t happens, and life throws a curveball at you with unexpected expenses. But you can prepare yourself for this by having the emergency funds we discussed. You can start planning them by starting your savings plan or starting to create a budget that includes them.

The money you set aside for the *curveball* can be kept separate from your savings accounts and can be kept primarily for any emergencies. You can name it your emergency funds to ensure you don't spend it on anything else except emergencies. You can add money to this account every month, even if it is just a little bit, or you can stop when you reach a certain amount. But whatever you choose, ensure you use it for nothing else except emergencies.

A WEDDING

You might not be close to ready to think about a wedding, but it's worth noting that it is an expense most people have in their lifetimes. You might not need to prepare for it right away, but remember that as you get older, chances are you're getting closer to having a wedding. And unfortunately, the wedding industry is exceptionally expensive. The costs of the venue, food, attire, decor, music, and drinks all tend to cost thousands and thousands of dollars. The statistics show that millennials and Gen Zs are having smaller weddings that are less extravagant and expensive, which is great! But it doesn't mean it will be cheap. Once you've started saving for other items and you've been able to achieve certain milestones, you can consider starting a savings account for a wedding.

ACTIVITY

Take some time to look at these big expenses. Which ones are you looking forward to the most? And do you have a plan yet for how you're going to fund these purchases? You can use this excitement to fuel your motivation to start budgeting.

You've made it so far! You're almost done, and then you can start taking everything you've learned and implementing it in real life. There aren't a lot of teenagers who take the time to plan their financial future, so you can take great pride in the fact that you're almost finished with this book.

This determination to get started with financial success is a great trait to have—don't let go of it. You're going to do so well!

Let's recap everything you've learned in the previous chapters.

SPREAD THE WEALTH!

You may not have the cash to share around just yet... But you do have knowledge – and you can spread it!

Simply by sharing your honest opinion of this book on Amazon, you'll show other teenagers where they can find this essential guidance... and that's a huge act of service you'll be doing.

Thank you so much for your help. Let's share the lessons the schools will never teach!

CONCLUSION AND REVIEW

Everything you've learned in this book can be put into practice in your teenage years and all the years to follow.

The information you've learned was intended to lay the foundation for a successful financial future. You have everything you need to set yourself up for nothing but growth, potential, and success. Whatever you learn about finances going forward can be built on this foundation—which makes for a solid beginning.

So, what did you learn in these chapters that you have to keep with you? Let's revise:

GOAL SETTING

- Setting goals is the first important step in financial success.
- It's important for you to work toward something while also ensuring you stay on track.
- Your goal has to include a plan, timeline, and regular revision.
- Staying motivated means you continually remind yourself of your goal so you can keep going when it gets tough.

GETTING YOUR OWN MONEY

- There are many ways you can earn your own money without having to rely on your parents.

Some of the best ways to make money as a teen include:

- Get a part-time job.
- Do odd jobs for neighbors.
- Start a small business.
- Have a yard sale.
- Invest money in bonds, stocks, or other investments.
- Sell items you make or find.
- You can also make passive income. It may take some time initially to get started, but it will pay off in the long run.

Some ideas for passive income include:

- Starting a YouTube channel that pays once you reach a certain amount of view time and subscribers.
- Affiliate marketing, which is when you receive a percentage for each item you promote and sell.
- Tutoring, which is ideal if you're good at a certain subject.
- Doing extra chores around the house, which your parents are willing to pay you for.

BUDGETING

- It has several benefits that lay the foundation for your financial success.
- You can't track what you don't measure, so start by tracking your current situation first.
- A budget should include your income and expenses, with allocated amounts for each of your spending categories.
- Your budget ensures you stay within your means, can track your money, avoid overspending, and can put money into savings.

There are a few budgeting mistakes to avoid:

- Making tracking hard.
- Expecting it to always be the same.
- Not constantly revising the budget.
- Not budgeting for fun things too.

SAVING

- The earlier you start saving, the better you'll be off financially.
- There are different ways you can save money in different areas of your life.
- By saving money early, you'll be able to fund unexpected expenses, build self-reliance and build stability for the future.

To save money, you should:

- Start with a plan.
- Open a savings account.
- Start with small amounts, which make a big difference.
- Invest in yourself.
- Save for your future as early as you can.
- Live below your means.
- Save your change to see how small amounts make a huge impact.
- Shop around for deals.

COMPOUND INTEREST

- Compound interest is often called the 8th wonder of the world since it's a powerful tool to dramatically boost your wealth.
- Compound interest lets you earn money on your money—so the more you have, the more you'll make.
- The earlier you start, the better off you are since the compound interest builds like a snowball.

You can start making compound interest work for you by:

- Starting early, even if it's just a little.
- Reinvesting your interest and never withdraw money from the account.
- Investing more money whenever you can to allow the money to grow faster.

KNOWING HOW TO INVEST

- Investing is one of the smartest things you can do with your money and is one of the most powerful ways to grow exponential wealth.
- Investing comes in different forms, from owning stocks to bonds and real estate—each with its benefits.
- It's important to remember that the value can rise or fall with investments, which is why it can be risky but also highly rewarding.

- There are many tools and apps you can use to not only start investing but also monitor it.

As a teen, you can already start investing in different types of investments, including:

- **529 College Savings Plan** – here, you can take advantage of tax deductions to help save for college.
- **Roth IRA** – which is a great platform to start saving for retirement and reaping tax benefits too.
- **Stock Market Index Fund** – which is a simple way to get started with investing in stocks.
- **High-Yield Savings Account** – where you build much higher interest than a traditional savings account, allowing for more compound interest.
- **Yourself** – which means reading books, taking courses, and taking care of your physical well-being. All of which will make a huge difference long term.
- **Real Estate** – which is where you buy a property that can be rented out for profit or sold later for a higher price than you bought it.
- **Emergency Fund** – which is crucial for anyone. It allows you the freedom to pay for unexpected emergencies without having to go into debt.
- **Forex** – which is the buying and selling of currencies based on whether their value will rise or fall.

As new investors, it is easy to make beginner's mistakes. So avoid those mistakes by:

- Not focusing on the short term but remembering that most investments are long-term based.
- Letting your personal feelings about a company decide whether you'll be investing or not.

CREDIT CARDS

- Credit cards have mostly had a bad reputation, but they can be used responsibly.
- Credit is important for major purchases like a house or car, so you have to start working on yours.
- Credit is based on your personal credit score—s0 the better your score, the higher your chances of getting loans for major purchases.
- You can build a good credit score by opening small credit cards or accounts and ensuring you pay them off on time each month.

To ensure you use credit responsibly and don't sit with a mountain of debt, you should:

- Never spend more than you can afford, so use minimal of your credit.
- Try to keep your balance below 30% of your limit to avoid huge interest costs.

- Always pay your bills on time to avoid penalties and extended credit terms.
- Only use your credit for items you need, so split all your purchases into "need" and "want" categories.
- Cut out unnecessary expenses from your life to avoid using your credit card unnecessarily.
- Make a budget and stick to it the best you can to avoid using your card.
- Not be tempted by the rewards you'll receive for opening a credit card—it's how they suck you in.
- Shop around for the best interest rates and payback rates on credit cards.
- Have an emergency fund to pay for unexpected expenses—avoid using your credit for those.
- Avoid using your credit card for cash withdrawals since they come with extremely high fees.

TAXES

- Taxes are paid to the government to pay for things in society, like roads, schools, and hospitals.
- There are a few types of taxes, mainly based on what you earn, what you buy, and what you own.
- If you're earning money, you will have to file for taxes, so ask for guidance from an adult.
- Keep all your receipts and sort them each month to make filing taxes easier at the end of the year.
- Ensure all your taxes are filed on time to avoid penalties.

- While taxes are important for society to thrive, there are ways you can reduce your taxes through tax deductibles.
- Tax deductibles are items or expenses you can't be taxed on, which saves you money in the end.
- Some examples of tax-deductible items include:

  ○ Costs of college and related items.
  ○ Charitable donations.
  ○ Costs for buying a home.
  ○ Saving for retirement.
  ○ Medical expenses.

CRYPTOCURRENCY

- Cryptocurrency is a type of digital money that is not controlled or owned by anyone.
- It is gaining a lot of attention since there is a lot of freedom and security surrounding it.
- You can either buy cryptocurrency to use it for certain purchases or use it as an investment opportunity.
- Since the currency is gaining so much attention, its value keeps rising, making it great for investment purposes.
- There are thousands of types of crypto, so it is important to get to know them and invest in the ones that show potential.
- Avoid common investing mistakes by doing your research and getting to know all aspects of crypto.

Cryptocurrency isn't failproof, and there are many mistakes to be avoided, namely:

- Not doing your research well before investing.
- Not researching the fees involved.
- Investing with the hopes of making immediate profits.
- Not saving your password somewhere safe since it isn't easy to get back.
- Opening yourself up to scammers with online wallets.

ROOKIE MISTAKES

- There are a lot of rookie mistakes that are easy to fall into but will result in serious financial losses for you.

The most common mistakes to avoid are:

- Buying impulsively, whether it be small or large items.
- Putting off saving until tomorrow and thinking there will be a better time to start.
- Buying items without first comparing prices to find the best deals.
- Having memberships and subscriptions you don't use or don't add value to your life.
- Not checking for hidden fees with bank accounts, credit cards, or major purchases.
- Maxing out your credit cards—making it impossible to close them.

- Paying off the wrong debt first—and not prioritizing debts with high interest rates first.
- Not investing in your future and postponing your savings.
- Not paying off your debt as quickly as you can—resulting in high fees.
- Not saving for emergencies that can often cost large sums of money.
- Not tracking your net worth to monitor your financial success.
- Bumping up your lifestyle with each paycheck.
- Buying something simply because it is on sale—which doesn't save you money at all.
- Allowing money munchers in your life, which are items that aren't in your budget, but you make exceptions for.

RETIREMENT

- It's important to think about and plan for retirement as soon as possible.
- The power of compound interest is very apparent when saving for retirement.
- There are many ways you can earn extra money to put into a retirement account.
- The importance of saving early is that it will allow you to perhaps retire early or retire with more money.

RAINY DAYS

- Having insurance is a key part of adulting since it helps get you out of trouble and big expenses.
- Depending on where you are in life, you'll have to take out different types of insurance.
- As a teenager, there aren't many insurances that apply to you yet, but as you gain possessions, the insurance will be more relevant.

The most common insurances include:

- Health insurance: for medical expenses.
- Life insurance: for your loved ones if you had to die.
- Disability insurance: for if you can't work due to disability.
- Homeowner's insurance: to protect your house and possessions.
- Auto insurance: for if something happens to your vehicle in an accident.
- Travel insurance: for if you travel abroad and something happens to your health or possessions.

Insurance isn't always easy to understand. So some of the most common mistakes include:

- Not understanding your coverage.
- Not getting enough coverage for what you need.

- Getting too much coverage for things that don't apply to you.

MAJOR PURCHASES TO PLAN FOR

- There are going to be many major purchases coming up in your life, and the sooner you plan for it, the easier it will be to get it.
- Many of these items are optional and may come at different stages of your life, but it's worth knowing what to expect.

These major purchases include:

- Your own car.
- Your own home.
- Vacations.
- A pet.
- College tuition or a gap year.
- Personal items: phone, clothes, and laptop.
- Your first investments.
- Unexpected expenses.
- A potential future wedding.

FINAL THOUGHTS

Now you are equipped with everything you need to get started on an incredible financial journey. You have what it takes to make an enormous success—you just have to believe it. And with this foundation, you are sure of nothing but possibilities! It is possible to become a millionaire with a normal job by using these strategies and sticking to them.

Can you see how these basic principles will set you up for a solid financial future? Can you see how implementing what you've learned here can help create the future of your dreams?

Not only do you have the knowledge to be in better control of your money, but you've also learned how to cut your current expenses while finding ways to increase your income. And best of all, some of the topics covered here will teach you how to make money without having to do much.

That is all you need to know to be in control, how to make more, spend less, and have money for the future.

There is so much to worry about in life, both as a teenager and an adult. And one of the last things you should have to worry about is getting by in life. More time should be invested in teaching teenagers about managing money. More effort should be put into teaching adults how to pay off their debts. And more enthusiasm should be poured into teaching everyone about the importance of starting young to be prepared for when you're old.

It is my biggest wish that this book covers everything you need to get going. And if you haven't started yet, this is your sign that you should. Right now.

RESOURCES

Websites for Learning about Investments

- Investor.gov
- Teenvestor
- How the Market Works

Brokerages for Opening Your First Investment Account

Keep in mind that these are designed for teens but will still need parental consent.

- Greenlight
- Fidelity
- Interactive Brokers

Opening Accounts for Cryptocurrency

Keep in mind that these are designed for teens but will still need parental consent.

- Flyte
- Early Bird
- Stack

Credit Options for Older Teens

While you need to be 18 to have a credit card, you can start building good credit with the help of your parent's accounts.

- Blue Cash Everyday
- Chase Freedom Unlimited
- Citi Simplicitiy

REFERENCES

Adams, R., & CPA. (2022, January 24). *How to Invest as a Teenager or Minor [Start Under 18 Years Old]*. Young and Invested. https://youngandthein vested.com/how-to-invest-as-teenager/

Allen, C. (2022, September 19). Cryptocurrency 101: A Guide for Parents and Teens. Mydoh. https://www.mydoh.ca/learn/money-101/investing/cryp tocurrency-101-a-guide-for-parents-and-teens/ Ancajas, J. (2022, May 6). How to save money as a teenager (& never go broke again). Mosdotcom. https://www.mos.com/blog/how-to-save-money-as-a-teenager/

Author, G. (2019, January 14). How to Explain Blockchain Technology to Your Children. CoinGape. https://coingape.com/how-to-explain-blockchain-technology-to-your-children/

Boggs, C. (2017, June 2). How to Teach Kids About Insurance. Www.iamagazine.com. https://www.iamagazine.com/magazine/issues/2017/june/how-to-teach-kids-about-insurance

Budgeting Tips for Teens in 6 Easy Steps. (n.d.). Better Money Habits. https://bettermoneyhabits.bankofamerica.com/en/personal-banking/teaching-children-how-to-budget

Cheung, K. (2018, January 19). The Beginner's Guide To Cryptocurrency And How Teens Can Benefit. WABE. https://www.wabe.org/beginners-guide-cryptocurrency-teens-can-benefit/

Connick, W. (2017, November 2). Your Teenager Should Have a Retirement Account. Here's Why. The Motley Fool. https://www.fool.com/retire ment/2017/11/02/your-teenager-should-have-a-retirement-account-her.aspx

CPA, C. R. (2020, December 31). How Much Does the Average American Pay in Taxes? The Motley Fool. https://www.fool.com/taxes/how-much-does-the-average-american-pay-in-taxes/

Cruze, R. (2020, February 25). How to Set Financial Goals. Ramsey Solutions; Ramsey Solutions. https://www.ramseysolutions.com/personal-growth/setting-financial-goals

DiLallo, M. (2015, January 31). Investment Guide for Teens and Parents with

Teens. The Motley Fool. https://www.fool.com/investing/how-to-invest/investing-for-teens/

Eli. (2021, March 8). 10 Things Teenagers Waste Money on. Teen Finance Today. https://teenfinancetoday.com/10-things-teenagers-waste-money-on/

FERNANDO, J. (2022, July 19). What Is Compound Interest? Investopedia. https://www.investopedia.com/terms/c/compoundinterest.asp

Fidelity. (2022, May 10). 5 Money Mistakes Every Teen Makes (and How to Fix Them). PureWow. https://www.purewow.com/money/money-mistakes-every-teen-makes

Financial Terms For Teens. (n.d.). Www.firstcomcu.org. https://www.first comcu.org/post/financial_terms_for_teens_to_know.html

Frankenfield, J. (2021, February 18). Bitcoin. Investopedia. https://www.investopedia.com/terms/b/bitcoin.asp

Frankenfield, J. (2022, May 28). Cryptocurrency. Investopedia. https://www.investopedia.com/terms/c/cryptocurrency.asp

FUSCALDO, D. (2021, August 16). Retirement Without Savings? Investopedia. https://www.investopedia.com/articles/personal-finance/111815/what-retirement-will-look-without-savings.asp

González, M. E. (2022, February 8). Easy Passive Income Ideas for Teenagers in 2022. Career Karma. https://careerkarma.com/blog/passive-income-for-teenager/

Grobler, E. (2022a, June 20). Investing Guide for Teens (and Parents). The Balance. https://www.thebalancemoney.com/investing-guide-for-teens-and-parents-4588018

Grobler, E. (2022b, September 13). What Teens Need To Know About Cryptocurrency. The Balance. https://www.thebalancemoney.com/what-teens-need-to-know-about-cryptocurrency-6281125

Grossman, A. L. (2021a, March 8). Short-Term Financial Goals for High School Students (26 Examples). Money Prodigy. https://www.moneyprodigy.com/short-term-financial-goals-for-high-school-students/

Grossman, A. L. (2021b, March 15). 9 Reasons to Save Money as a Teenager (Use these Talking Points). Money Prodigy. https://www.moneyprodigy.com/reasons-to-save-money-as-a-teenager/

How To Make Money As A Teenager: 25 Lucrative Ways. (2021, August 11). Clever Girl Finance. https://www.clevergirlfinance.com/blog/how-to-make-money-as-a-teenager/

https://www.facebook.com/thebalancemoney. (2022). Teens and Income Taxes. The Balance. https://www.thebalancemoney.com/teens-and-income-taxes-2610240.

Joy, D. (2015). How To Set Financial Goals: 6 Simple Steps. InCharge Debt Solutions. https://www.incharge.org/financial-literacy/budgeting-saving/how-to-set-financial-goals/

Knueven, L. (2019, July 15). The 7 most expensive things you'll ever pay for, according to financial planners. Business Insider. https://www.businessinsider.com/personal-finance/most-expensive-things-americans-will-pay-for-2019-8

Lake, R. (2022, May 23). A Guide To Making Money as a Teen. The Balance. https://www.thebalancemoney.com/how-to-make-money-as-a-teen-5323084

Lobell, K. O. (2020, October 15). Money Foundations for Kids: Compound Interest. MoneyGeek.com. https://www.moneygeek.com/financial-planning/compound-interest-for-kids/

Mint. (2021, March 29). Budgeting for Teens: 14 Tips For Growing Your Money Young. MintLife Blog. https://mint.intuit.com/blog/budgeting/budgeting-for-teens/

Money Management Tips for Teens. (n.d.). Credit Counselling Society. Retrieved December 15, 2022, from https://nomoredebts.org/budgeting/budgeting-for-teens

MSc (Econ), E. O. (2021, January 9). 35 Simple Ways To Make Money as a Teen in 2022. Savvy New Canadians. https://www.savvynewcanadians.com/make-money-teenager

Muller, C. (2021, November 22). How To Save Money As A Teen - Money Under 30. Money under 30. https://www.moneyunder30.com/how-teens-can-save-money

Mydoh. (2022, September 19). Budgeting 101: A Guide for Parents and Teenagers. Mydoh. https://www.mydoh.ca/learn/money-101/money-basics/budgeting-101-a-guide-for-parents-and-teenagers/

Nielsen, K. (2020, February 10). Blockchain 101. Blockchain Education Network. https://medium.com/blockchainedu/blockchain-101-b62cf28997f3

Richmond, S. (2019). Why Save for Retirement in Your 20s? Investopedia. https://www.investopedia.com/articles/personal-finance/040315/why-save-retirement-your-20s.asp

Sabrina. (2020). 9 Powerful Benefits of Setting Financial Goals - Finance Over Fifty. Ramsey. https://financeoverfifty.com/benefits-of-setting-financial-goals/

Segal, T. (2022, January 27). Why a Tax Credit Is Better Than a Tax Deduction. Investopedia. https://www.investopedia.com/terms/t/taxcredit.asp

Union, A. F. C. (2022, December 7). 5 Major Life Purchases to Plan For. www.amerfirst.org. https://www.amerfirst.org/blog/post/5-major-life-purchases-to-plan-for

Wei, J. (2022, September 19). Common Financial Literacy Terms for Kids. Mydoh. https://www.mydoh.ca/learn/money-101/money-basics/common-financial-literacy-terms-for-kids/

Yoder, T. (2022, April 19). 10 Essential Tax Savings Tips for Small Business Owners in 2022. Fit Small Business. https://fitsmallbusiness.com/business-tax-saving-tips/

RESOURCES

Blue Cash Everyday® Credit Card | American Express. (n.d.). Americanexpress. https://www.americanexpress.com/us/credit-cards/card/blue-cash-everyday/

Chase Freedom Unlimited Credit Card | Chase.com. (n.d.). Creditcards.chase.com. https://creditcards.chase.com/cash-back-credit-cards/freedom/unlimited

Citibank Online. (n.d.). Www.citi.com. https://www.citi.com/

Credit Reports and Scores | USAGov. (n.d.). Www.usa.gov. Retrieved December 20, 2022, from https://www.usa.gov/credit-reports

Earlybird. (n.d.). Early Bird. https://earlybird.com/

Fidelity International. (n.d.). Www.fidelity.nl. Retrieved December 20, 2022, from https://www.fidelity.nl/

Greenlight Invest Overview. (n.d.). Greenlight.com. Retrieved December 20, 2022, from https://greenlight.com/invest

Home | Investor.gov. (2019). Investor.gov. https://www.investor.gov/

How The Market Works. (2019). Free Stock Market Game, Create Your Own Contest. Howthemarketworks.com. https://www.howthemarketworks.com/

Investing & Banking for Under 18s - Flyte.com. (n.d.). Flyte.com. Retrieved December 20, 2022, from https://flyte.com/

Lowest Cost Online Trading and Investing | Interactive Brokers. (2015). Interactivebrokers.com. https://www.interactivebrokers.com/en/home.php

Stacks. (n.d.). Www.stacks.co. https://www.stacks.co/

TeenVestor | Investing for Teens: Stocks, Cryptos, & Funds. (n.d.). TeenVestor. Retrieved December 20, 2022, from https://www.teenvestor.com/.

Nerd Wallet nerdwallet.com Retrieved February 6,2023, from https://www.nerdwallet.com/banking/calculator/compound-interest-calculator

Made in the USA
Middletown, DE
21 December 2024